EDUCATION AND THE SOCIAL CRISIS

KAPPA DELTA PI LECTURE SERIES

*

In the present volume, which is the fourth in the Kappa Delta Pi Lecture Series devoted to discussions of the broad meaning of education, Professor Kilpatrick analyzes with the meticulous care of critical reflection the social problems of the hour, and proposes an educational program that charts the way toward their solution. Not only is there need of a public school education that derives content and method from current social needs, and thereby quickens intelligent awareness of a citizen's responsibilities and promotes critical thinking concerning them, but equally imperative is an adult education that will continue such open-minded and shared group thinking whereby "the whole population, young and old alike, will be consciously studying to criticize and improve society at any point of possibility and always for the common good."

Education and the Social Crisis contains the essence of a social and educational philosophy based not upon absolutistic concepts of individual and society but upon pragmatic experience, that is, upon the reality that challenges and tests individual and group intelligence here and now. It is, therefore, a most timely volume. Professional educator and layman alike will find herein the specifications of a new education, continuous as life itself, and concerned with the vast coöperative project of social reconstruction through intelligent planning.

EDITOR.

EDUCATION

AND THE SOCIAL CRISIS

A PROPOSED PROGRAM

*   *   *

BY

William Heard Kilpatrick

**PROFESSOR OF EDUCATION, TEACHERS COLLEGE
COLUMBIA UNIVERSITY**

LIVERIGHT PUBLISHING CORPORATION

NEW YORK

PRINTED IN THE UNITED STATES OF AMERICA
BY VAN REES PRESS, NEW YORK

FOREWORD

*

This little book is a call to the teaching profession. Given as a single lecture, it can, even though here enlarged, lay no claim to economic or other completeness. Its effort is to summon the profession of education to a study of the stupendous task now looming before us as our civilization faces perhaps its greatest turning point in modern times.

Some will probably object to certain of the things herein said. Such is to be expected, but whether critic or criticized—or neither—be right, the confronting task and call remain. The profession of education must think through these problems and go on thence to meet its inevitable duty. Only as we think in new and better fashion can we hope to discharge that duty. A broader and deeper conception of the work of our profession must result. Nothing less will suffice.

To name my indebtednesses would make a list too long for the output. One, however, must be mentioned. In the study of this topic I owe much to a series of discussions held with a group of my colleagues. These have helped me to see the problem more adequately and so the better to weave the fabric of thought herein presented.

W. H. K.

Sept. 1, 1932.

CONTENTS

*

CHAPTER I

THE TASK AND PROBLEM

*

THE world of affairs is profoundly disturbed. Momentous social changes seem in process. Civilization confronts epoch-making decisions. Education must face this situation and act appropriately. As we look beneath the surface, what deeper character do we see in the confronting situation? What becomes thus the task and duty of education? These facts and these questions set the problem for this study.

That great changes are going on under our very eyes, every one can see. Even the youngest and most careless reader will admit it. But there is more to be said. Not all is well. With all our boasted progress, things seem to be turning out in not the right way. The ills from our present serious business depression, serious as they are, are in themselves not so significant as what they reveal. The very foundations on which we have been trying to build our economic civilization stand challenged as apparently inadequate to carry the load we had put upon them. Must we lay other foundations? Other times have known their business depressions, some more severe in certain respects even than this, but never before have so many thoughtful people questioned so deeply. Never before, in this country at least, have so many so openly questioned, for example, the actual basis and organization of our economic system. "Social planning" is the new term on many lips. At the least, this means a conscious and

3

ordered departure from *laissez-faire;* at the most, it cuts much deeper. However viewed, the inherent working of our industrial system seems of itself to call for its own re-ordering. To let things drift is but to compound disorder. We dare not. But the task is great, none greater has this country ever faced. And the responsibility rests on us of this generation. The future of our country lies in unique degree in our hands.

As we face this economic responsibility, what of education? Can it remain as now? Is it right to bring up the rising generation as if nothing unusual were happening? As if they would find the same world that we found—or thought we found—when we were growing up? We cannot, we dare not, so treat the youth committed to our care. Such a course would be as unwise and unkind as it would be futile and false. Any system of education must always confront life itself. As life changes, so must the system of education change. But more than this, education must actively help to remake life. In fact, education taken in the broad is but society at work consciously remaking itself as it remakes its circumstances. In order to answer, then, for a newer education we must ask more closely about the situation which confronts us.

CHAPTER II
THE SITUATION NOW CONFRONTING US

*

HOW shall we see the situation which now faces us? Do current events in fact challenge the existing system? What is the bill of particulars? While full treatment lies, of course, beyond this little book, we can at least demand to know the crucial matters involved. Wherein does our new industrial society disappoint us? What seems fundamentally wrong?

THE PASSING OF THE OLD FREEDOM

OUR first disappointment attaches to the oldest American hope, to what some have called the American dream.[1] From early days onward this country has meant to give to every man, especially to the plain man, a chance to fullness of life denied him elsewhere in the world. Our dream has been of freedom, that no caste or hereditary privilege should deny opportunity to any, that every one who would honestly and seriously try might here find freedom and opportunity to work out his own life by his own effort and according to his own planning—achieve economic security, live reasonably well, serve as a worthy and effectual citizen, educate his children and see them well set upon the same road toward a like successful life. Freedom and the promise of success upon effort were per-

[1] See James Truslow Adams, *The Epic of America*, pp. 404ff. Boston, Little Brown and Co., 1931.

haps the two ideas that most often came to mind as our pioneer fathers talked over such matters.

This freedom had many aspects to the early American, but none sweeter than the opportunity as an individual to map out his own life—choose his occupation and change it if he wished, choose where he would settle and change that too if he fancied. And all the time to run his own life to suit himself, asking permission of none other. Such freedom was, of course, at bottom dependent upon economic opportunity, and this was then given in the abundance of new rich land available for settlement. In those earlier days, it was measurably true that whoever had the will might hope, as they said it, to "succeed." And the ideal has entered deep into the American soul. No story has been more often applauded than that of the poor boy who has won success by his own honest hard work against untoward circumstances. We have cherished the belief that we were founding a nation and a society in which such "success" should always be thus open to individual will and honest endeavor.

How has our growing industrialization affected this cherished American dream? For a long time the old faith still held amid the new conditions. Our bias, after the manner of cherished beliefs, made us fasten attention upon the favorable instances, upon the many great successes achieved from humble starts amid the new industrial opportunities. The list of such was in fact impressive and we easily ignored the many who under the new régime were being tied down to the control of others. We forgot that "success" under the new conditions was generally if not necessarily based upon a real exploitation of many others. America was still the land of golden opportunity. American wealth had become a proverb the world over. We were proud of our achievement. If we ever thought of the many being submerged, there seemed a way out.

Did not statistics show an ever advancing standard of living among ever larger numbers—more telephones, more bath-tubs, more automobiles, more radios? The showing was rosy. Many enthusiasts more recently claimed that we had achieved a new economic system in which stocks would forever go up and all might own. We had only to buy ourselves rich.

One thing, however, could not be permanently ignored, and that stands out to distinguish the new order from the old. Our depression has taught it to the dullest. For the many, the old individual freedom of opportunity to initiate has gone. The old individual independence has given way to our present corporate dependence. Once any able-bodied man could find work if only he would. Now it is far different, work is no longer at the individual's will. It is given or withheld by the whole great impersonal aggregate of affairs, and this—so far as the individual as such can do anything about it—works apparently without rime or reason. "Market conditions" rule. No entreaty, no command, no device has so far sufficed to change the Juggernaut course of these. In those old days while commerce and market conditions—and land speculation even then—brought a certain amount of wealth, the mainstay and ultimate reliance was the individual farm supplemented by the local mill. To a degree beyond the conception of most now living, human wants were cared for in the home and neighborhood. Life was simple to be sure, hard and meager, most would now think, but such as it was it lay within the control of individuals. In essential degree, economic security and individual liberty did lie in individual hands. Now the picture is far different. Modern wealth is increasingly a matter of mass production. Raw materials are brought from many widely separated quarters and the finished products are sold over ever increasing areas. The new order joins together ever larger

7

numbers of people from increasingly widespread areas into ever growing inter-dependence. And over it all and in it all "market conditions" do in fact hold sway. Each year it becomes truer that men may now work only as this impersonal great industry grants them opportunity. In the highly industrialized nation the worker is swallowed up in the all-devouring whole. The old freedom is gone.

Individual welfare, individual opportunity to work, effectual individual liberty—name it as you will—all this has become thus dependent upon the successful working of our aggregate economic machine. In a new sense and degree we are all bound together. In older words, the cause of one is the cause of us all. In a still older phrase, we are all members one of another. And this is literally true. We have in fact a common fortune. We all are alike dependent members of one economic régime.

THE BREAKDOWN OF OUR ECONOMIC MACHINE

AND how does this new industrial order, this economic machine, work? The answer is on every one's lip. At times it works flourishingly. At other times, like the present, it refuses to go. And this refusal seems strange beyond words. We have produced so much of wheat and cotton and oil and coal and manufactured goods that we cannot sell. We therefore cannot buy. So we suffer amid plenty. Because of our very abundance of production, we have breadlines, men clamor for work, mills stand idle. We all suffer. The longer our economic machine refuses to go the more we suffer. Probably it will soon start again, but even so it will again break down. Thus does this cruel, blind, and fitful machine control us.

What is the matter with the machine? Why will it not work? Again does full discussion lie beyond us but some things must be said. And also again, the situation seems strange beyond words. This machine which has thus become the sole reliance for our whole, inter-dependent economic welfare is not run with the intention of caring for this welfare. In essence it has a different intent or, perhaps better, many different intents. The theory underlying our economic régime is this: That any group which can by hook or crook get control of any part of the economic machine shall use that part for their selfish advantage, running it without regard for the rest and primarily to extort as much as possible from the rest. Each such group literally and precisely—so far as intent goes—thinks only of itself and of what it can get. What may happen otherwise is not its concern. The wonder is that such a machine will run at all.

HOW MODERN INDUSTRY TIES US TOGETHER

But there are yet other surprises. When any object to the way in which the machine works and begin to ask embarrassing questions, we hear a very odd kind of answer. We are told that this war of part against part is the good old American way of granting to each individual his freedom of initiative and opportunity—the basis, these people go on to say, of all our success and greatness. They call this our "rugged individualism."

There seems here somehow a fundamental contradiction between the lauded individual freedom and initiative on the one hand, and the actual opportunity for the individual under conditions of mass production on the other. Let us examine into the matter. Take any of our mills as an example. Ford and Carnegie and Schwab are indeed outstanding instances of individual initiative and success. In a sense such an opportunity may yet be open to any, but is it in fact open to all? Consider any plant as a whole. It is a corporate affair. In it many men must work together. What proportion of the men can exercise freedom and initiative? What proportion are hired and fired as "market conditions" dictate? And even when "times are good" and the economic machine runs well, what proportion of the population can by exercising initiative map out their economic life as they will? Does not the very conception of mass-production (at least as hitherto regarded) mean that only the very, very few are free in the old American sense to carve out life and fortune as they will?

And the difficulty here is inherent. In order to have mills there must be more workers than managers. Always so. These workers, of course, may have the freedom of leaving one mill and going to another, but seldom more. In effect they are tied down to the acceptance of rule from outside themselves, of taking what the mill will grant. That old American freedom of choice and action was based on small farms or small industries where the owner was free to do pretty much as he would with his own, and the hired man could have real hope that if he cared he too might come to own and direct and so himself be free. And there was land enough then available for these conditions of freedom to be realized. All the hired men could so hope. The prospect held literally for all, even for all at one and the same time. But how is it now under modern mass production? Can each of all Ford's working men reasonably hope to start such a factory for himself? The answer is a clear and necessary no. There cannot be enough new mass production factories for each man later on to have one such of his own. It is an impossible conception. As soon, then, as America began with factories, the old individualism itself began to go. What was left of initiative and freedom, in the old economic sense, became reserved for the few who could become owners, managers, bankers, and the like. The rest (as things are now run) must be hirelings and dependents, more or less docile parts of a great unmanageable whole. The proportion of our population now found on payrolls tells the tale. Except for a minute few, those now on payrolls must stay on payrolls; and there—as matters now stand—they are not free, but dependent on others, but most of all dependent on "market conditions," on the blind workings of the great economic machine.

But some will ask, what about people not connected with factories? Are not the farmers, for example, as free as ever they were? And what about small shopkeepers and individual artisans and professional men, lawyers and doctors? Space forbids full examination, but let us at least glance at the farmer. Is he now prosperous? Surely and obviously not. In fact, in our modern bad times farmers seem somehow to suffer first and most. How are these things so? Whatever else be true, as soon as the farmer begins to buy manufactured articles he too enters the industrial system. He cannot buy from the system unless he sells to the system, and thus he too becomes entangled in the system. He rises or falls, as does the system. And so it is with all the others. In one way or another the whole country now depends for its well being on the good working of industry, on the success of the industrial system as a whole. Look about now and see who are not hurt by the depression. The cobbler perhaps prospers, because more people than usual are wearing patched shoes. But the proportion of hurt to not-hurt tells the tale. As a population we are indeed all tied together.

But even this is not all. We still have the injustices of distribution. Our present economic practice is, to state it baldly, that in any mill, after the laborers have been paid as little as it has been possible to pay them, all responsibility to them ceases. Good times and big dividends carry no responsibility for lean years—beyond building up reserves to care for lean-year dividends. In bad times, the

men may be turned off freely. Whether dismissed workers starve concerns the workers themselves and by
chance a humane public, but it is no concern of the mill—
nor (apparently) of the Federal government. What such
a custom must mean in insecurity and bitterness of soul,
in personal demoralization—supremely important as these
are to our problem—we shall not here discuss. The economic unwisdom of the custom, however, has begun to be
questioned. Whenever any one of the warring parts of
our economic machine turns off its men, the other parts
suffer because men-out-of-work cannot buy. So other warring parts must shut down, and then still fewer men can
buy. A bad condition grows worse. If somehow workers
had assured pay-checks, sellers might have assured buyers,
and business could plan assuredly. Apparently, then, we
manufacture our own depressions, and—many begin to
think—perhaps needlessly.

THE NEED FOR A PLANNING ECONOMY

THUS come about such suggestions as the Swope plan,
the plan of the National Chamber of Commerce and
others, for unemployment insurance, regulation of wages,
vocational reëducation and the like. It begins to seem
plausible that since good and regular wages would mean
more buying power, good and regular wages might in the
long run mean more and better business. In such ways
does even business itself begin slowly to see that we do
in fact all hang together, and accordingly must somehow all manage together if things are to go well.

What some have been praising as "rugged individualism" begins thus from many angles to look not so much
like the old American freedom for all as rather a contest
among economic higher-ups, as to who under the new
conditions shall control and exploit the rest of us. Since

we are in fact all bound economically together, does not our social task begin then to emerge into clearness of obligation? Must we not first of all see to it that our inclusive economic machine shall in fact work,—not break down every few years? And even more if possible, must we not further see to it that our industry be not a mere Juggernaut machine but a system—a consciously managed system—which shall work intentionally for the welfare of all? And also whole-heartedly for the good of all, and not do this as now only accidentally and incidentally while intentionally it is working for the aggrandisement of the few? So to change affairs that these ends be attained, this is the great social opportunity that calls to the men and women of this generation.

When we look, then, at our present hard times, it appears, so to say, that we deserve what we are getting. We have not seriously tried to improve things. There is no such thing as total over-production, it is simply bad proportion in production. If only we produce in proportion and distribute appropriately, the more we produce the more we shall all have. And there is no end to the possibilities. The sober calculations of engineers assure us that were our mines and farms and mills but properly proportioned and then run to capacity we could easily abolish all poverty, abolish much if not most of present illness, give economic security to all,—during sickness, in old age, during expectant childbirth, during technologic unemployment. Some have gone on to calculate that, granted the proper management, it would be possible to reduce work to 4 hours a day, 5 days a week, 30 or 40 weeks a year, for a working lifetime of 25 years, and yield to each family the equivalent of say $20,000 a year. We may doubt specific figures, but the general picture remains. We are worse than stupid not to study the situation. Prob-

13

lems there are and problems there will always be, with difficulties attendant. But intelligence and the stout heart exist to use on problems and difficulties. Our fortune still lies in our own hands if we will but coöperate to attack the problem.

THE PROFIT MOTIVE AND HUMAN NATURE

POSSIBLY at this point we should discuss a formerly accepted doctrine which now remains with many as a hindering superstition. Is man selfish in all that he does? Is the profit motive so inherent in human nature that it must forever remain the principal if not the sole motive of human action? Many answer yes to both questions, especially as regards the masses of men in economic affairs, and conclude accordingly that our profit system, being thus imbedded in human nature, is here to stay. To question it is, to those who so hold, but folly or worse. What are we to think?

That man, economically speaking, does now work largely from the profit motive—and many, if not most, selfishly so—may well be admitted. As long as the competitive profits scheme is the universal system under which we all live, it becomes in fact practically impossible for the vast majority to fail to act from the profit motive. Under such conditions we should expect the motive to become established and the many to become selfishly self-centered or family-centered in their economic outlook. We can then argue that the profit motive and attitude which now we find so prevalent are the effects of the profit system, not the cause of it. And the history of the doctrine tends to confirm this view.

When the *laissez-faire* position was young and flourishing, Bentham (1748-1832) and James Mill (1773-1836) thought to build an ethics and a psychology to fit it.

14

Adapting an older way of thinking they put forward pleasure or happiness as psychologically the sole end of effort. So well did this fit the *laissez-faire* outlook that many accepted it—for a while. But a closer analysis shows that men entertain many varied ends, that action is the effort to attain them, and that happiness is a result attending success in connection, seldom a direct and actual end in itself. Competent thought has so accepted for now a half century, Thomas Hill Green (1836-1883) summing the conclusion perhaps best. And analogously for the doctrine of universal selfishness, though latterly some have tried in vain to revive the view in connection with a mistaken denial of choice. Probably the fact of complexity of motive will best explain the confusion. Ordinarily each one acts from a variety of motives. The mother, for example, will dress her child partly for his comfort and well-being, but also in part to impress other mothers and so exalt herself. The convinced advocate of the selfish happiness view seizes on this latter element as the essential factor at work, calls it the sole end of human action and counts the child welfare motive as means to it. We have, however, no difficulty in finding instances where this so-called sole motive nearly, if not quite, disappears and the other motive clearly asserts its dominant position. We see this with any true mother when her child is seriously ill. History shows the same thing again and again, as in war and in times of persecution, when some at any rate have gladly given their lives to further their cause. To say that these people were simply seeking happiness and were selfish about it is both to miss the point of life and to empty good words of their appropriate meanings.

As regards, then, any claim that the profit motive is so inherently imbedded in human nature that it must forever remain the dominant reliance for human action, the facts are all the other way. Psychology, as we have just seen, denies it. Indeed, it is not psychologists who nowadays thus reason about elements fixed beyond change in "human nature," but principally advocates of otherwise losing causes, such as retired generals and R. O. T. C. officers trying to bolster up such things as preparations for war— in general, convinced advocates seeking a short-cut answer to otherwise difficult arguments. History abundantly refutes the inherent profit motive claim. The position falls down not only in those cases where one gives his life for his cause, but even more to the point in the early tribal life where all pursued in common the tribal enterprises. To say that these are instances of the profit motive working not in behalf of the individual but of the tribe is to yield the whole point at issue, for in this tribal life the individual tribesman so worked for the common good, so lost himself in the common cause, that he literally could not think himself apart from the group. During most of his life on earth man has worked best when lost in common tribal causes, giving up any possible personal gain for the welfare of the whole. And the common run so felt and acted. A group spirit was built to demand it, and the demand was met.

To say that the profit motive is instinctive and must remain our sole or even principal reliance for human action is thus to deny the most obvious facts of human conduct and history. No theoretical obstacle prevents effectual coöperative action. The tribesmen got such action. Had they been sophisticated their reactionary opponents of change would have declared coöperation fixed indelibly in human nature. The problem then is practical: how to break the stranglehold of a competitive system which requires men to work against each other to their real hurt instead of working together for their truer good —and teaches them so. Men can learn coöperation or they can learn cut-throat competition. It is the system now in

16

vogue which teaches the latter, and men thus learn it. A coöperative system could as well teach coöperation. Tribal life so taught and succeeded. We face then not a theoretical problem of whether it can be done but a practical problem of how to do it. The profit motive is no instinct, it is not fixed in human nature.

CHAPTER III

ATTENDANT EVILS OF OUR PRESENT SYSTEM

*

SOME perhaps have been wondering whether education had dropped out of our inquiry. Economics we have had —too much, these may think—but what about the school? Where does it come in? Even yet, however, we are not ready for the school. The situation demands further analysis. And in this analysis education will appear—an inherent and anti-social education—but the school as such we must still postpone.

The essential civil war of part against part within our present industrial system brings with it other profound evils, not in themselves economic, but largely social-moral. Chief among these perhaps stands, as suggested above, an anti-social mis-education of our people. And these social-moral evils appear to be growing, possibly most of all in our own country. To make matters still worse, part of the attendant mis-education so closes the minds of our people that any widespread, fair appraisal of the situation seems so far impossible. Multitudes living thus in our present system and habituated to it, have come to think that the system and its resulting motivation are inevitable in the nature of things and inherent in fundamental human nature. To question these things seems to these people impossible and absurd.

Let us look first of all at some of the general social-moral conditions of our times and our country. The view is not reassuring. We had the Harding régime oil scandal, in which one very discouraging feature was the strenuous and widespread effort of others—public leaders included—to deny and hide the facts. And more discouraging, if possible, was the further widespread public indifference to the disclosures as finally made. As if to balance this scandal, there are now being disclosed in the chief city of our country abundant evidences of pervasive political graft, met again with astonishing indifference and even cynicism on the part of the public generally and by actual vociferous support on the part of the fellow members of the Tammany political group. Meanwhile business shows its own graft and corruption. Racketeering disgraces our cities. Kidnaping abounds, harrowing at times in the last degree. Crime flourishes, having become, some say, no longer a profession but an occupation supporting perhaps a million of our citizens. Figures in this field are, of course, notoriously unreliable, but it does appear beyond question that many of these evil conditions are appreciably worse here than in any otherwise comparable country. Just how far these moral evils do result from our bad economic system may, of course, be questioned, but the conditions fairly considered seem to substantiate the position here taken.

THE MIS-EDUCATIVE EFFECTS OF OUR BUSINESS SYSTEM

It appears that the fundamental conflict within our economic system discussed in the preceding pages creates also a fundamental and inherent moral conflict within modern social life, and these two conflicts account in large part for the bad moral conditions. Modern industry, as we have seen, ties us together. Intelligent morality would demand, then, that we face this situation and work together. But business still follows the idea and practices of

19

an earlier day and each man in intent works only for himself. A clear conflict thus ensues. All the obvious and immediate rewards follow business and the older outlook. The welfare of society demands the new outlook. As might be expected, the obvious and immediate rewards prove more appealing for the large majority, and none possibly escape altogether. Educative effects necessarily follow the effectual appeal—it must be so—and character is built accordingly. The sober conclusion seems to be that the American character built by its own inherent processes fails further and further to meet the new demands. Three lines of failure are noteworthy, first in respect of a general public spirit necessary to the working of democratic institutions; second in the matter of honest dealings, especially where public interests are involved; and third in the matter of parasitic gain. The last named may require a word of explanation. Consider as an extreme instance the matter of professional gambling. Why is this not counted a socially useful occupation? For one thing, it is a demoralizing influence. In the worst cases, its devotees will no longer work at useful employment, they will steal if gambling fails them. In other words, they have become truly demoralized. And lesser devotees show the same only in lesser degree. From another angle, such an occupation performs no social service. Those who live by it are economic parasites. They live off society. They give in return no *quid pro quo* of social service. Under modern industrial and economic conditions the growth of legally permissible parasitic gain, especially in the form of speculation and high power promotion, has become demoralizingly great.

These three lines of growing breakdown in the moral structure of society so act and interact together that in practical effect they are hard to distinguish, nor indeed is it necessary to do so. How the general bad moral effect

20

results from the conditions, that is what concerns us. Consider first the matter of public spirit. It is notorious how little continuous effort is put upon affairs of public concern as opposed to private interest. Hardly half of our people take even the pains to vote. When an intelligent foreigner asked a New York business man why the bigger business men did not unite and clean up the city, the reply revealed probably the true reason: "It doesn't pay to give the time and effort to it, we can make more by attending to our private business than the politicians and grafters will steal from us by their increased taxes and bad politics." In other words, the rewards from private gains appear so much surer and so much greater, at least to the many, that they give all but exclusive attention to their private interests. The essential point here to be noted is that our system of rivalry for gain virtually hires the people not to give attention to matters of public concern but instead to give it exclusively to their own private affairs. And the general public approval of success in business matters is so great that the young are potently educated to accept this indifference. So strong is this influence that few can escape it. The greater the possible rewards and the greater the popular approval the stronger the probable influence on the many. And again does educative effect inevitably follow effectual influence. We may argue or preach against these ill effects, but until conditions are changed we cannot hope for different results. Under modern conditions, since we are more and more interdependent, the demands of the public welfare are far greater than formerly. But as matters now stand the effectual rewards and actual approval work increasingly in favor of private interest against the public welfare. The results we see on all sides.

But this is only a beginning at the needed analysis. The bigger and more complex our business organizations become the more the opportunities grow for parasitic gain and the easier to disregard the hurt done to others by dishonest practices. Speculation gives perhaps the clearest instance of both of these evil results. In ordinary speculation, certainly the one who gains has given no *quid pro quo,* no more than does the gambler. He has got something for nothing, and the demoralizing effect may be as great. Along with speculation go also all those forms of doubtful and evil promotion where the main intent is to "unload" on an innocent public. And along with these come all that more respectable control over combinations by bankers and capitalists where little or no service is given for the profits extorted. Possibly the most demoralizing feature of all this is the great stakes held before the young as possible to be won by rendering thus this worse than no service. In this country the cream of our youth in untold numbers are being allured by the hope of such rewards to give themselves mind and soul to this pursuit of parasitic gain either directly as managers and speculators or indirectly as lawyers or engineers or salesmen to serve them. All of these are thus educated and paid to use their talents not to help society, but in fact rather to live as parasites upon society. The money that has been lost in wages and investments since October, 1929, is some indication of the direct and indirect cost of this parasitic incubus. The moral and intellectual cost is incalculable. The possibilities of such gains and the study and attention given to securing them have educated possibly a controlling fraction of our people to look upon factories and business enterprises not as servants of society to meet the legitimate wants of people, but rather as stock market counters whereby those who succeed with these counters may contrive, wring out, extort profits for themselves in entire disregard of cost or injury to others. The strategic influence on the public mind of such successes increases the pernicious effect of these practices beyond any computation. As long as these ideas and the people who possess them thus control our society, just so long shall we all suffer. These words must not be understood as meaning that some among us—the rich, for example—are sinners above all others. It is the system which is to blame and we are all caught in it. We all share more or less in the support of the system. It appears, indeed, that certain of the great managers see and deplore the evil workings of these things better than do the majority among us. And how does this bad education affect affairs?

The principal ill effect is possibly this. The bigger and more complex business becomes the harder is it to see connection between cause and effect, to feel the connection between conduct and its result. When the stock market goes up, where does the new wealth come from? The question is so difficult to answer that few think to ask it—such connections are simply ignored, "What is it to me?" these say, or "I should worry." The more people who come thus to think of such gain, the more there will be to disregard the means used for acquiring it, the more who will think that "only saps work," and consequently in general the more who are morally weakened. Thus results an ever growing population who continually demand to get something for nothing, with many among them willing to get this something at any cost to others. It is but the worst specimens of these who become professional grafters, racketeers, kidnapers, hold-up men. These criminals are simply the worst fruits of a widespread demoralization. For each criminal there are many near criminals and for each of these a still larger number of loosened moral stamina and outlook—and in some measure at least all these mutually encourage each other. Meanwhile it is our system that has made them so and is still making others like them. As with all educative effects, the results are inherent in the system itself. We must blame the system, not its victims. Most of all we must blame those among us who, knowing better, still uphold the system.

It is in the light of such an analysis that we must consider the oil scandals, the political corruption, and the widespread graft. These are but the inherent educational results of the possible high stakes on the one hand and the difficulty of seeing and feeling cause and effect connections on the other. Home and school and church may succeed in teaching the old-fashioned honesty of the simple face-to-face kind. Few among us steal actual coin in hand or actual goods in store. But there is another kind of honesty, not so easy to see. While home and school and church have been teaching the old and simple virtues, life all about us has been teaching our young people that "success" is the chief end of man, success that is in the great struggle at rivalry for gain. And this same all-pervasive life early tells these young people—as soon as they enter business if not earlier—that honesty must not be taken too seriously lest success be jeopardized.

When the young and the privates in industry hear of the great rewards that so often go with crooked practices among the captains of industry, there easily grows the cynical belief that "they all do it." "Sure, each man gets his, that's how people get on, you'll never get rich any other way." The more we study speculation and its schemes of promotion, the harder is it to draw any satisfactory line between speculation and speculative promotion on the one hand and racketeering on the other. Each is trying to get something for nothing. All such practices belong essentially on one scale, whether legal or illegal. The bad educative effect of the legal may in fact be the greater because the more insidious. Getting something for nothing at the expense of others is socially evil and wrong, however it be named. It is this which demoralizes. And at bottom lies rivalry for private profits in the face of conditions that tie us together.

AMONG these various ill results some call for particular attention. Political evils are blatant. The connection here with our economic system seems to be this: Business interests wish special favors from government and, caring only for profits, will be willing to pay for the favors at the cost of corruption. Some officials, also putting gain first, will contrive to sell the favors sought. Shrewd politicians, likewise concerned first with personal gain, will build political machines to facilitate this buying and selling. The public, in its turn, engrossed in private gain, will disregard the public welfare, continue to "vote straight," and thus maintain the machine in power. We find here an interlocking series of vicious circles. Dishonest business will corrupt officials. Corrupt officials invite more of such dishonest business. Such buying and selling degrade political organization into the corrupt machines we know. Corrupt machines in their turn invite corrupt business and provide the needed corrupt officials. A public which has become discouraged and cynical at past reform failures renounces politics as too dirty to touch and turns to more complete engrossment in its own selfish efforts—the crux of the trouble from the first. The picture here is of local politics. In federal affairs it is rarely the corrupt official. Rather is it the log-rolling for special interests, lobbies, veterans' organizations, members seeking reëlections, interested voters back home seeking their personal gain, with the spoils system as the special disgraceful link between federal and local political machine.

Sickening as is the thought of such things, we can have little hope for substantial improvement so long as each

25

person's direct and strong interest is felt to lie in his own affairs in opposition to that of all others. So long as we have to live under such a system, we must expect such educational effects as these practices on the one hand and this public indifference on the other. Only the few can be expected to resist the demoralizing effect of the selfish struggle for gain; the many will yield. Where the treasure is, there the heart will be; and thus will follow accordingly this public mis-education of character and will.

PERSONALITY AND LIFE SUBORDINATED TO GAIN

A FURTHER mis-educative result is the built-up disregard of the worker as a person. So long as production is for profits only and it is counted right to pay labor as little as possible and deflect all else into dividends, just so long are the employer and owner educated by the system they accept to look upon the workers essentially as means to producing dividends. It has been so in every day and time: when men treat the worker as means only and not also as end they degrade him, they treat him as less than a full person. This was the sin of slavery. In lesser degree only it is the sin of our present system of economic control and distribution. Witness the twelve-hour shift of the steel workers, since given up, and ponder the arguments formerly used in advocacy of it. If democracy means anything, each human must be treated as a person, not as a mere instrument of production to the advantage of others. Here, fortunately, business itself begins to join hands with democracy. It becomes increasingly recognized that we cannot dispose of the goods made unless all the people, including, therefore, the workers themselves, share more fully and equitably in the profits. Only thus will there be sufficient buying ability to take care of what is produced. Dividends must include workers as truly as owners

26

and managers, or the economic machine will not run.

In close connection lies another evil of which at least passing notice must be taken. Its adequate discussion would ramify practically into all else. In running industry for profits only, we have usually forgot that working is itself a true part of life. Faithful to our unfortunate *laissez-faire* theory, we have expected from industry to get money and then with money to buy life—or pleasure, as that theory called it. And the results are what might have been expected. In tendency at least, none connected with industry have lived except after the hours of work. All in modern industry, a few perhaps at the top excepted, have tended to find the labor not sufficiently varied or meaningful to be satisfying. Salary and wages have accordingly gone for excitement to even up the boredom of mill or office. Money has bulked so large that we have lost in life. It will be a vital part of any new civilization to ask first and all the time about life, that it be as good and fine for all as we can learn how to make it. And life cannot in the long run be either good or fine unless it be rich in variety and meaning. In particular, a man's work must be meaningful to him or life suffers. Man's life consists not simply in the abundance of things that he has, his heart must go fully into what he does and he must lose himself in it if he is in fact to find the goodness of life.

THE SYSTEM DEVELOPS A DEFENSE MECHANISM

As we think of improving life through any better social and economic arrangement we come to face a further evil attendant upon the existing state of affairs. Those who count themselves to profit by the existing state of affairs, and in our country they are many, tend to wish it kept unchanged, and accordingly are averse to having its shortcomings discussed. This is not to accuse any of deliberately hiding the truth, nor is it to say that only the rich count themselves to profit by the existing system—either statement would be too naïve and simple to make or accept. It is rather this. Whoever accepts any state of affairs whatsoever to live by it with no incentive felt to question it, such an one so long as he so feels comes by an inevitable psychological effect to "believe in" that state of affairs. Living by this state of affairs and believing thus in it, he is very likely—unless he has broadmindedly studied the history of such things, to think it dangerous, and so wrong—to question such a state of affairs. And the more surely any one profits by a system the harder is it for him to accept arguments against it. This is the history of the Tory mind, the social Fundamentalist, everywhere and in every age. Our time is no exception.

In such ways does it come about that the public mind is kept as far as possible off such fundamental matters as the needed remaking of our economic system and turned instead to such safe commonplaces as bringing back beer or electing the next president or praising a woman for an Atlantic flight. The effect of such withdrawal from fundamental matters is everywhere bad, but worst, possibly, in our schools. We have almost no school attention given to the study and criticism of our vital social questions. So much has education been counted to be a mere indoctrination that all the stereotyped defenders of the social *status quo* have insisted that only the hitherto accepted ideas be mentioned before pupils. School thinking becomes thus too often utterly inane, and teachers too often the most timid of professional workers. That education is primarily an affair of getting young people to think better than hitherto and desire better things and that teachers must lead in the process—such ideas have been quite taboo. Accordingly we have the super-patriots insisting on indoctrination not only in narrowly conceived patriotism, but

28

as well in *status quo* social and political doctrine, and equally bent on excluding any questioning attitude at all. All such is, of course, simply an education into the ostrich-like attitude of hiding the eyes against impending danger,—the worst possible preparation for intelligent action. Our present bad condition is but eloquent testimony to our inadequate thinking.

CHAPTER IV
IS THERE A WAY OUT?

*

IT would be only futile thinking to analyze a situation and then do nothing about it. We must do more. We must go as far as we can along the road toward a solution. What are the steps to be taken?

THE MORAL OBLIGATION INHERENT IN THE SITUATION

IF we accept the analysis as above made, the economic situation defines the moral obligation of to-day. We cannot avoid it. The people of this country must recognize the economic and social facts and plan accordingly. Otherwise they are recreant to their moral obligation. It was of the essence of our analysis that planning is the way out, such planning as offers a continuing intelligent attack upon the essential evils disclosed. We must, it appears, move toward a dual balance, the one balance within production itself that each part may fit and support the rest, the other balance between production and distribution that the two may fit appropriately together. Only thus can we produce to capacity, only thus can all we produce be sold. To effect such coördination, we must recognize that competitive rivalry, whatever may once have been true, no longer suffices,—that this rivalry has now in fact become the chief evil. Furthermore, the planning and the balancing we seek must be done, consciously, for the public good, and ultimately under public control. And strategic as the economic situation may be at the present it is not the whole. Intelligent study must concern itself with all that makes life good. As fast as such planned economic support and security is won, can we move on hopefully to the further and richer things.

HOW SHALL WE PLAN?

WHO are to plan and how? Where is the leadership to come from? And what part has the profession of education in the matter? Speaking for myself, I do not know just how the planning is to go on and I know that I do not know—I am not expert in such matters. I feel sure, however, that much institutional reorganization is necessary. As for the profession of education, I conceive it to have a real share in such planning, but by no means to carry the whole of it. And I further conceive that the planning is to be done democratically.

Many will at once ask about these things. How can education share in such leadership? How is this leadership conceived, and how the education? And how does democracy enter? How can democracy and education and leadership be as intimate as seems to be implied and the planning process still be efficient? These questions raise crucial points and we must face them.

First as to democracy and efficiency. It must be admitted that many are questioning the current working of political democracy, and this not without reason. It seems clear that some new institutions of social control must be devised to take account of the new conditions. Some accordingly are looking toward Russia and others to Italy. We should study Fascism and Communism, they may have suggestions for us. But adopting is another matter. Of all things the pursuit of efficiency must be realistic. It must take the actual facts into account if it would produce real effects. First of all, as we have already seen, at least part of American political inefficiency finds a prior cause and explanation in our bad economic system. If business on its bad side would but keep its evil hands and influence off government the success of our democracy might be greater. As an experiment this might at least be worth trying. But, further, we are trying to run twentieth-century industrial, urban America on an eighteenth-century plan of government devised for a sparsely settled agrarian country. Only romance could expect such an effort to succeed, and especially so since ours was the first, as modern man began to remake governments, to meet the democratic demand. This first model is now clearly out of date. The typical American of to-day demands the latest model motor car, but he still holds to the actually oldest model among modern governments. When it rattles or breaks down, he should not be surprised nor refuse to admit the fact. Still less should he object if the rest of us complain. But even closer to the point at hand, if it comes to changing our social affairs, it is neither realism nor efficiency to expect America in trouble to think first of revolution. Violence, true enough, is easy for us. Resort to lynching is certainly all too frequent, but a violent overturn of government is a very different matter. America will not begin to set her house in order either by calling for or by accepting a Lenin or a Mussolini. Such things might be tried as a last resort, after many other things had failed and matters were still getting worse; but first, never. Moreover, if matters should get thus finally worse, employer Fascism would be far more likely than a proletariat dictatorship, but even this only under the guise of a constitutional emergency measure. America believes very fundamentally in constitutional government.

Whatever, then, is to be tried in this country must expect to capitalize the deepest in American tradition, and that is constitutional democracy. But in order to succeed, this democracy must be willing both to clarify the vision of its aim and to experiment with new means. We must see with clearer eyes the confusion into which our out-worn institutions have brought us, and we must be willing to devise new institutions to control our marvelous new agencies of production. And still further, if this situation is really to be met, we must devise these new institutions for the good of all and not for the good of some against the rest. And the planning and the accepting of plans must both somehow remain in the keeping of the people—we have too much at stake. Some may not like these limiting conditions, and they may say they will not work. But the realistic thing is to accept conditions as they are and try what can be done within them. So much for a democratic start.

The problem of leadership is more difficult. The various demands seem incompatible. The people—including those ordinarily called leaders—are in confusion. They demand better times, but they still hold to the same old ways which brought on the bad times. They require leadership, but they know not whom or what to trust. They do not know what to think, but so far they seem not willing to study, and "the leaders" again perhaps least of all. If we depend upon present leadership, it appears that we shall drift—a most vicious counsel of despair, to be avoided if it possibly can be done. Is there a way out? Where is the needed leadership?

DEMOCRATIC LEADERSHIP DEMANDS SHARED SEARCH

THE leadership which promises best for long-run efficiency seems to arise from the fullest group sharing. This is so contrary to widely held views that we must consider the matter closely. Let us look at it first in the small. Suppose a dozen men about a table working at a matter of common concern. How does the process of shared search go on, and how does leadership function? All share in the discussion. What one says stimulates others to new and better thought. One proposes a plan. It is considered. Bearings are noted which the proposer had overlooked. The plan is amended. Still other bearings are noted, and still further amendments. If actual progress is made, interest will grow. All work with new zeal, each from his peculiar background and experience. Out of such variety comes discriminative criticism. So the men work together, now this one advancing the process, now that one. They seek a plan which shall integrate what all know and feel. A better plan should result than the best man acting alone could have produced.

LEADERSHIP THREE-FOLD

WHAT now do we mean by leadership? What different kinds do we see here at work? How do they mutually support each other? Let us think of leadership as the proffering of any step or movement which does in fact advance the process under way. It will be interesting to see in such an instance as that just set out how large a proportion can share in one or another kind of leadership.

The first leadership is that of interest, the sense of a confronting evil or difficulty with concern that something be done about it. With our twelve men some first felt such concern. They talked about it. The idea grew. In general this stirring comes first from those who now suffer from the bad state of affairs, or at least in some who work with these. Seldom will the sense of concern arise from those who profit from the evil state of things. History

34

and psychology are very clear here. The favored ones seldom propose reform.

The next leadership probably is that which works with men and affairs,—in the large we should call it statesmanship. When men of this kind had been enlisted in the cause, they began positive steps. A meeting was planned. Their adherence gave status to the movement and a third type of leadership, men of expert knowledge, were induced to join.

Actual conferring brings inter-stimulation. Proposals come best from the men of constructive thought, but they are criticized by all, especially perhaps by those who know the bearings in their own lives—even the humblest can help here—and by those leaders of men and affairs who are sensitive to the practical workings of things on popular psychology. It takes all types to carry the process forward to a satisfactory conclusion.

LEADERSHIPS ARISE WITHIN THE SITUATION

THE points most to be noted in this analysis are that leadership is many, not one, and that each leadership by its own step forward mutually brings the others into fuller being and action. Also, that the leadership of interest and concern is as true a factor of success as any other, and that the interested group develops, from within, its other needed leadership—history has often noted this with surprise. Note in all of this the widespread sharing. All may share in the factor of interest and most, if not all, in the criticism—and in so doing even the ordinary man may really contribute. This is by no means to disparage the factors either of expert knowledge or of native gifts. Each leadership, in fact, is an essential condition of the common success. Each contributes uniquely. The analysis, however, does tell us not to think of leader and led as a final distinction fixed in advance independently of the matter at hand. Interest, experience, and expertness differ as truly from topic to topic as they do from person to person, and actual leadership is not only varied but is properly developed on each occasion out of the peculiar conditions there obtaining. Leadership is essentially a group achievement.

This kind of process where all share responsibly in the search, where there is the freest possible interaction and inter-stimulation among the members of the group, where each proffered contribution is judged exactly on its inherent merits and not on the status of the proposer—this is what we mean by the democratic process at its best. That the process is also a mutually educative one is equally true and by the same analysis. On this must be built our subsequent educational program. That the varied, needed leadership is developed in and through the process we saw above. In fact it may be said—and almost as a truism— that leadership and plan are emergent products of the same successful search. If anything comes first it is intelligent interest. To help build this interest in any one connection is peculiarly the educational function. Thus it appears that, education leading, any and all may contribute to democratic leadership and democratic planning.

CULTURAL ACHIEVEMENT A GROUP PROCESS

THE analysis just made receives further support as we consider the analogous development of the great cultural achievements of history. Where a great work has been done no single person has done it, but many. It is often said that later generations stand on the shoulders of their predecessors. The figure speaks the truth but not the whole truth. The fuller process seems much the same as that studied above, only more widely extended both in time

36

and in numbers concerned. It may well be that a whole people—in the effectual participation sense—may labor for generations. Where such determined interest dominates, the results at any one time will be the survivals of many offerings and of continual criticism. Successive efforts give examples of ever higher achievement. Successive criticisms have raised ever higher standards. Public approval has stirred and sustained the effort and rewarded success. In this way is genius aroused and directed. In like way is expert knowledge made increasingly better. In a true sense, the whole (effectual) people working together have achieved the final result. Here as before there have been various leaderships—genius and expert knowledge among the rest—and each has in its turn stimulated and sustained the others. Among them, popular interest and concern has here been a true causal factor. In a true sense, a whole people working together, perhaps for generations, has achieved the result.

To analyze thus the process of cultural achievement is not to say that we can control the process at will. Actual achievement is highly complex. Ancient Greece achieved greatness in philosophy, art, and literature, but could not achieve a lasting government. Italy succeeded in music and art over Great Britain, but Britain has surpassed in statesmanship and government. France, perhaps best of all, exhibits all-round success. Germany has succeeded in music and scholarship, but has so far failed in art and government. It does, however, appear that each such success is a group achievement extending through generations, and quite possibly the greater the proportion of the achieved mutual interaction within the otherwise participating group the greater has been the success. Music and art in Italy would illustrate the positive of this, and historic German government the negative.

AND what now of the social-economic situation confronting us to-day, the case for leadership in the large? If success is to follow effort here, must we not expect that in this case as in the small, there will be the varied leaderships and these must by their mutual inter-stimulations bring each other into adequate action? It is hard to see how success at shared search in such an inclusive cause can be attained unless at least a working majority of our people are enlisted in the conscious effort, and the more so enlisted the better by much. Otherwise the search and consequent program will lack the dominant supporting interest necessary for success. Nor is the quest without hope.

Already the depression has made people question our economic arrangements as never before. Already capable students have proposed promising plans, as also have men of affairs. So far, however, any widespread effectual understanding is lacking. Demand for positive action there might be, if only the people could see clearer what to ask. But till now they think in the old terms. They still cling to the impossible individualism of the past. That all can prosper together they still cannot accept.

Education to see the situation in new and better terms seems the present need. Successful leadership thus to see may hope to arouse the leadership of popular conscious demand for the needed shared search. Once the problem is clear and the search is on, the process becomes easier. Experts in the field must lead the people to an understanding study of the situation and then of proposed ways out. Such a study should be educative in the best sense and again mutually inter-stimulating, though we expect the experts to be real leaders in the study. Since the whole people are

38

involved, the leadership of men in the large, or statesmanship, will probably be needed to help the people give sustained attention to essentials in the face of both conscious and unconscious attempts at confusing the issue.

Whether the shared search will in fact conclude for planning belongs, of course, to the future. The only basis of expectation lies in the use of intelligence. In the degree that our own analysis has been founded on intelligent study, in like degree may we expect further intelligent study to confirm it. If planning be accepted, a program must be worked out. A gradual introduction of planning would seem probable. Mistakes will be made along the way—that is to be expected. But granted a sufficiently determined and intelligent interest, continually increasing success is reasonably to be expected. Such an interest seems the key to the situation. Given that, the rest can hardly fail to follow.

SOME POSSIBLE LINES OF PLANNING

WHILE it does not belong here to map out planning procedures, a few words to indicate possible lines of thought may help the further discussion. An inclusive national planning board of the highest professional standing would seem necessary. This should have governmental connections but need not, to begin with, be an exclusive governmental agency. A semi-independent status might make it easier to secure from learned bodies their best personnel, while it may well be that an advisory function is as much as can be got at the first.

Such a planning board should have the right to call for help upon the appropriate government bureaus and departments,—the census bureau, the departments of agriculture, commerce, labor, etc. That the freest interchange of opinion may operate throughout, there should be organized state and local coöperative planning groups; and effectual communication should be established with any and all groups of interested citizens.

A proper survey of existing facilities of production and of probable needs should, for one thing, furnish a basis for public advice as to the fields of proper and improper investment. There are far-reaching effects possible here. What changes we shall ultimately need to make within or away from our present capitalistic régime may be argued, but for some time to come sound advice on investments will prove a welcome business asset. An association of bankers working in connection with the planning board could simply by advice and publicity against speculative excess of capital investment go far not only toward remedying some of the present worst abuses of unbalanced production but as well help greatly in the spread of educative thinking on the necessity of balancing production both within itself and against probable needs. This kind of planning will win an initial support from many conservative business interests who otherwise might fear the whole idea. And in connection with thinking about such there should gradually emerge the necessary conception that our several welfares are in fact all tied together, that *laissez-faire* has now broken down, that we must in self-defense seek the common good.

But planning, of course, will be equally concerned with the other side. A better distribution of income must be effected, else we stay where we are with all the present injustice and insecurity and besides cannot sell what we produce. When recommendations for such better distribution of income can come from the highest authority, officially recognized as such and working clearly for the good of all, and will specify the specific procedures, it will be easier for the proper public interest to arise and act. In connection also the whole problem of employment will have to be faced,—its better distribution, unemployment insurance, vocational guidance according to planning foresight, re-education following technological unemployment, etc., etc. And again can the actual work of planning and the discussion that goes with it serve to educate broadly both as to the need of planning and the procedure for effecting it. In such ways can a beginning grow, grow educatively, into fuller and better planning as fuller experience and criticism can show the way.

DANGERS AND DIFFICULTIES

Suppose we achieve the interest and begin on the search, what chief dangers and difficulties will confront such an effort? The chief difficulty probably is the bottom cause of it all, namely, that our system is one of rivalry for individual advantage over others. This may be expected to hinder in at least two ways. It will so blind us that we shall hardly study with eyes or mind open to change; self-interest acts that way. It will further lead many who are fearful of losing their present vantage to oppose and confuse our study and search. And unfortunately our means of communication are largely in such thwarting hands. Another difficulty lies in the widespread inexperience of our people in sustained group thinking. Without such thinking we can hardly hope for that determined and intelligent interest which is necessary to sustain the whole enterprise. Again does education become our hope for democratic and efficient effort. Education must help us to open our eyes. Education must give us the practice in group thinking. A new adult education is an essential step in the process. And so we ask the next question.

CHAPTER V

WHAT SHALL EDUCATION DO?

*

A SURVEY of our progress will perhaps make clearer where education enters and how it can serve.

We have studied our social and economic situation and have felt insistent arguments for conscious planning if we are to realize what our new technology has to give us. We have found, too, that it is not simply economic good which is to be sought, great as that promises to be. Possibly the chief gain will be moral and social, that we shall cease our struggles to extort advantage each from the rest, with all the mis-education, the immoral and disruptive tendencies that go along with such efforts, and learn instead the team play of civilization. The direct and indirect advantages of such team play promise to be very, very great—not the least being that we can feel a feasible and necessary cause worthy of the best that in us lies. And in the pursuit of this cause we shall be working not against each other but together. All can help each and each all. The moral gain from such a state of affairs is so great as to be incalculable. Not since tribal life have morals and advantage been so thoroughly united.

We have found further good reasons for believing that in the long run the most efficient approach to this better state of affairs lies in the shared search; and that such a shared search gives all a chance at participation and even at leadership; and further that in such shared search the leadership of interest is perhaps most of all the strategic factor in sustaining the process: to call out the other necessary leaderships, to afford the conditions for their effective functioning, to supply the needed interested criticism, and in general to push the effort onward toward success. But such an interest cannot be effectual unless it is as intelligent as it is determined. Otherwise, the continuing process of eliciting and criticizing and accepting plans and programs can not be appropriately done, and standards of judging will not be reliable.

Still further, we found as underlying the whole process of shared attack that all the various leaderships, that of intelligent interest as well as the rest, do by their successful inter-active effect among themselves mutually bring each other into more and more effectual being and action. Such a process of mutual inter-stimulation and criticism, particularly as put upon the needed basis of intelligence, becomes precisely the educative process most truly and properly at work. We of education are thus inherently at home as we concern ourselves with such matters.

EDUCATION AND THE DEVELOPMENT OF INTELLIGENT SOCIAL INTEREST

IT is, then, exactly at this point of intelligent interest and understanding that conscious education can find its task and service. It must work partly in helping to develop, call out, encourage, accept, reward, expert pertinent knowledge—a most important kind of leadership. It must work chiefly in helping to build up in the people a general and intelligent interest in the problem at hand based upon an intelligent understanding of our situation: What is wrong and why; how planning is proposed and why; the best plans that have been proposed with their strong and weak points and why.

43

So stated education can be true to itself. Helping people to an effectual understanding need be neither propaganda nor indoctrination of any particular position. It can and should be genuine study and constructive criticism. Still further, helping people with interchange of views to study and think—and act accordingly—is not only education at its best; it is as truly our historic American democracy working at its best. The profession of education can then gird to the task at hand in full assurance that it is living up to the highest ideals alike of the profession and of historic America. But not to go thus forward would be to fail both.

THE PROFESSION OF EDUCATION AND ITS RESPONSIBILITY

EDUCATION, however, can hardly be true to itself or its obligations in any full sense unless it becomes in fact a profession organized and ready to assume its social responsibilities. To make this clearer the term education demands at this point consideration that we may distinguish from a narrower use here restricted to the profession of education, as such, a general use of the word as broad at least as thoughtful experience. From the broad point of view all life thoughtfully lived is education. To give conscious attention to what one is about, to seek and note significant meanings in what is happening, to apply these meanings as intelligently as one may to the direction of one's affairs —all this is not only the path of efficient dealings, it is equally the process of education in possibly the only full sense. So understood, every intelligent farmer, every thoughtful mechanic, while he pursues his specific efficiency, is at the same time educating himself in the school of his experience. But the farmer or the mechanic rightly thinks of himself not as an educator but as a farmer or mechanic. His education may be inherent in what he does

44

and it is true education, but to him it is incidental. Education as a process in and of itself and how to manage it as such is not his vocational aim.

The like thing holds, or may hold, in public affairs. When any group of citizens study, say, the working of their city politics and propose as a new venture a commission form of government and hold meetings to hear discussed the merits and dangers of the new proposal, real education is—or ought to be—in process. And, again, after certain ones become convinced that the new proposal is a worthy one, the best to them so far made for their city, and these undertake to persuade others to the like mind so that the proposal may be accepted at the polls, we still have what is—or again ought to be—a process of education. Here the attention given to education as such is, if properly done, rather more conscious than was true of the farmer or mechanic; so much so in fact that the process of study and subsequent persuasion is often called a campaign of education, though in the judgment of this writer such a campaign is not properly one of education in its best and truest sense except as there is real study of the proposal on its merits with real willingness to shift, accordingly, to any other position that may in the course of study appear the better founded. At this point the question of propaganda and indoctrination naturally arises, but discussion is reserved for later consideration. Here the emphasis is that any appropriate study and consideration of public policies definitely includes education in the fullest sense and may involve also the best intentional education of citizens. In the latter aspect we have moved beyond the inherent self-education of farmer or mechanic, but we still need not have in mind the study of education as such in its fullest sense.

The profession of education, as here understood, carries a step further the element of conscious study and responsibility. There comes a time in developing civilization when in a given society the possibilities of education have become so great that the matter cannot wisely be left to the incidental results of endeavors otherwise conducted. For the better direction of the social process itself, the study and practice of education, as such, must be set aside for special attention, and a particular body of citizens be made responsible for the proper pursuit of this study and for the appropriate application of its results within the social process. Thus is conceived the profession of education. It is, of course, true—humiliatingly true —that the historic beginnings of the profession, as often happens with origins, did not carry the significance sketched above. Too often has Bernard Shaw's gibe been justified, that "those who can, do; and those who can't, teach." Some one has even added that those who can't teach, teach how to teach. We may, however, now smile at these things and place such former schoolmastering by the side of the barber origin of modern surgery, for a new day dawns. Whatever may have been true in origin, it is by now becoming clear that in our day education is so significant in possibilities that we must constitute ourselves into a true profession, inferior to none, in order to take adequate care of our obligations. And, in the judgment of this writer at least, we must make this profession the responsible guardian of society's conscious and intentional education. Let the words, "the responsible guardian," be here noted and emphasized because much turns upon them. They constitute a noble charter and impose grave responsibilities.

What shall be the work of this profession? More specifically here, how shall it help our people in the social and economic situation now confronting our civilization? Several things can be set down in order:

THE PROFESSION AND EXPERT ECONOMIC KNOWLEDGE

FIRST in immediacy of connection with economic planning and with the task of helping our people to think about it is the obligation to help supply the needed expert knowledge. We have within our profession probably the chief economic experts in the country. These men must come forward as leaders to help plan and educate. They and other like experts must by no means allow so important a function as national planning to fall into the hands of mere politicians. For these seeing through the old eyes will still seek personal advantages to themselves and to their parties and sections. The planning we need must consider the public welfare as a whole. Probably no experts are so impartial, so truly public spirited, as the economists within our ranks. So much for the first step. This work is not so much the responsibility of the profession in its organized capacity as it is of some within our ranks while they coöperate on the outside.

THE NEED OF THE PROFESSION FOR A BROADER OUTLOOK

SECOND, considering the profession more narrowly as those consciously so organized, our beginning task is to take ourselves in hand. We must become socially minded and socially disposed. We must come to see jointly and severally that education and the social situation are so inextricably interwoven that we cannot truly educate except as we admit the social aim and responsibility and remake on this basis our whole school content and procedure. On the whole we are herein sadly lacking. Our teachers have thought not in terms of social responsibility but rather of subject-matter and mere school keeping. Our administrators have thought too much in terms of

47

bare business efficiency and administration and not enough of education and especially not of the possible social service of education. We shall not properly see or feel our specific task until we do so take ourselves in hand. We must all together study our social problems until we become fired with zeal for the cause of a better social day. We must commit ourselves and our work intelligently to the cause of the public welfare, not in lip service but in appropriate and effectual endeavor.

We must then openly assume our social responsibility. We must mean to help society, old as well as young, to move along most defensible lines to the ever emerging best social goals. As we seriously undertake this, we must expect to run risks and incur enmities. For as soon as we begin to be effectual we shall meet opposition. Fortunately for us, responsibility and interest will mutually build each other. If we begin where we are, both will grow. As we sincerely work, our effectiveness will increase.

Accepting thus our social responsibility, the charter of our social commission must be thought out into its manifold pertinent implications. This will require a new openness of mind. Old positions will often hinder. We must clarify the new vision. In particular, we must re-think in thoroughgoing consistency what the theory and practice of our education must be if our profession is to discharge its social obligation to society. And there can be no answer to such questions except as we study our actual social situation. We wish a new degree of coöperation, for example; we must then ask whether our marks and contests and prizes do not belong to the selfish rivalry which we are to put behind us. We wish a democratic social order, which means criticism and social judgment. We must then ask whether our textbooks and our recitations upon assignment do not make docile and thoughtless acceptors of the *status quo* rather than the thoughtful and

48

critical citizens needed to bring the better day. We wish citizens who will work for the common good. We must ask whether our school work, remote as it is from life, can be expected to build a regard for the common welfare. All these and much more must we study, if we are to make our school system effectual to bring the new day.

Finally, our task throughout is coöperative. All of these things must be thought through together by the various members of the profession. It cannot be the exclusive work of experts. All must coöperate in the mutual education, mutually stimulating and checking each other's thinking, mutually supporting each other in our endeavors. In two directions must we work, the one to build up the profession from the point of view of organization, the other to build up the individual members. Organization we shall need to speak suitably for us before other groups, particularly as our members meet opposition for doing their duty. The public mind needs educating as to what open-minded study means. Our progress here should be wisely gradual, but advance we must continually make. Organization will be necessary. We must also build up ourselves individually, for the work at hand is at the bottom to be done by intelligent individuals, whether as teachers or officials. But we shall not get intelligent teachers and officials nor will they have the adequate encouragement and opportunity except as we all become socially intelligent and socially disposed together. The profession must take itself in hand. To reëducate ourselves to the new vision is our first great step.

THE PROFESSION'S RESPONSIBILITY TOWARD ADULTS

THIRD, we must inaugurate an epoch-making system of adult education, newly conceived to meet the actual confronting situation. Nothing less than a new epoch will serve. Adulthood is two-thirds of life, surely it is worth at least half our educational efforts.

Mere school education cannot possibly suffice for the whole of life. To think otherwise is to misconceive and belie the very meaning of education in relation to life. Education goes on as life goes on. Life is a novelly developing process. It does not repeat itself. In certain older and static civilizations, one generation did perhaps so repeat preceding generations that education could apparently be repetitive and transmissive, but for us even this appearance has long passed. Modern change in very significant respects defies adequate foreseeing. Mere analysis of what is, with consequent fixed-in-advance solutions, no longer suffices. Education is most truly conceived as being life itself creatively facing its novelly emerging problems. Under such circumstances education must continue all through life. We need, then, a new type of adult education, thoroughgoing, widely-inclusive, ever-continuing. Only on this basis can modern civilization hope to meet intelligently its problems.

Existing adult education is, of course, tragically inadequate. The name we brought over from Great Britain, where it began for the under-privileged. As at present conceived, adult education discusses its problems in such terms as "culture," "vocation," "parental education." These are all good. They enter properly into the whole, but unless we can see this whole more fundamentally, more inclusively, our work along these separated lines is wholly inadequate. It can easily be misleading.

The essential aim for the matter immediately at hand is that our whole people may come to an intelligent understanding of our social and economic situation. We saw above how such an understanding is crucial in any hope for better things: how understanding leads to interest and search, how widespread intelligent search calls forth and criticizes both planning and leadership. We seek in the new adult education this strategic understanding and interest. In particular, must a wise adult education make for that intelligent and critical interest which we saw earlier to underlie all efforts at economic improvement. If shared group thinking is to be possible, this is the place of all others where we of the profession of education can best help.

What we wish is that the great body of adults, even if they hold college or university degrees, shall seriously study our social order and its possible improvement in all significant aspects: how inefficiently we produce and why; how unjustly and inefficiently we distribute and why; how badly our political system works and why; how much better our economic needs might be cared for; what rich and happy living for the individual calls for and how this good life needs study that we may really use art, music, religion, to make life better; how, on the one hand, all these are now largely on an exploitation basis as through them men seek to exploit others for gain, and how, on the other hand, they are largely on an "escape" basis as through them we seek to forget and escape life. We must further study honestly and openly what other peoples are doing to help themselves—the Russians under Communist leadership, Italy under Fascist rule, city housing in Vienna, the many insurances to be found in Europe, and in them all the bad as well as the good and why. These are but samples of what the new adult education must study. Nothing human shall be foreign to it, but all will be studied that together we may open our eyes and see. We must build a more intelligent understanding of what we have and why, and what we might have and how.

Some may question whether our adult population can be expected to come to any effectually new understanding.

Are not present ideas and attitudes fixed already beyond changing? That there are difficulties here none can deny, greater perhaps than most who urge the point see. If people think with the ideas they now have, how then can thinking give new ideas? If people evaluate with the values which they now accept, how then can the using of present values lead to new values? In other words, we confront the question of helping people to find a new and better philosophy and whether such is possible. And therein lies the rub. Philosophies seem to show the same instinct for self-preservation popularly ascribed to animals. They hold on to life, some of them, as has been said, even after their brains have been knocked out. But as history tells us, people do change their philosophies. Even if we do think with existing ideas, we change these somewhat as we try them out on new situations. Deep changes may come slowly but they do come. At times, however, the change is more rapid. By all the signs we are living at a time of such rapid change. The new industrial régime has introduced so many necessary changes in living that philosophy cannot but be affected. Science helps. And just now, perhaps most of all, does the depression. In its urgency our people are in fact questioning as never before. As long as the depression lasts, at least so long will serious questioning continue.

When we think of those adults now in charge of affairs, it does appear that they need, perhaps most of all, a new philosophy of life in place of the old and decaying philosophies that most now have. We can no longer be content with mere production of goods. We must ask what it is all for and whether a better outlook is not possible, and how we may perhaps found a new society on a new ethics and a new goodness of life. Hitherto our effective social philosophy has been a *laissez-faire* seeking of selfish good with the implied acceptance of the *status quo*. We have.

on the whole, refused both for ourselves and for our children any careful criticism of our social institutions in spite of the obvious evils thus perpetuated. We have actually fought against both criticism and change. We have conducted nationwide contests on the federal constitution as if to make sure that our pupils should more surely accept that document as sacrosanct, beyond recall. Are we never to face realities and think fairly and honestly with ourselves and children? We must awake to the fact that life, or civilization, is in process, that except in death it never returns upon itself, that change is the most significant modern fact, that intelligence must re-found itself on the situation as it is and its becoming as the only hopeful basis for making it better. A new fundamental outlook is needed in place of the old if we are to go ahead smoothly. A chief duty of adult education lies just here.

It is, of course, true that as soon as we begin to discuss such criticism and change, even with adults, oppositions will arise. These are to be expected and it will be the part of wisdom and duty not to offend unnecessarily. We seldom anger people into fruitful study, and this fruitful study is always our aim. For the sake, also, of the new school program we must have the parents go with us. And this will come to pass if only we ourselves but do our part. Tact and an honest wish to help, with a sincere willingness to learn as we deal with others—these things must characterize our new adult education.

Where shall we first look for support and acceptance as we undertake such a system of adult education? The answer would appear clear. We must begin with the broadminded. Fortunately the number of these seems increasing, especially so in our days of adversity. In openmindedness our women, it appears, often surpass the men. Business tends to close the minds of the men, women are less immediately caught in the system. The League of

53

Women Voters, the American Association of University Women, the better of the women's clubs, here present opportunities. Next, perhaps, in open-mindedness come the under-privileged. These are on the whole possibly more interested in economic matters than are their more fortunate fellows. This has been the rule of history, those who have more fear more. "Let well enough alone," they say. On the other hand, those who have little to lose have little to fear. They are more open to new thoughts, and many too have already been doing a great deal of good thinking. There are dangers here, of course. Those who stand to gain may over-rate a proposal of change, just as those who stand to lose may under-rate it. What we wish, if we can but get it, is to have differing initial attitudes come together in one group. As best we can we must seek the fair appraisal from the point of view of the common good.

What machinery is needed for the new adult work? No clear answer can be given now. This remains to be worked out. If we bring together the extension course idea, the seriousness of the British Workers' Education Association, and the discussion group procedure, we shall probably be looking in one direction of fruitful experiment. Apparently there must be city, state, and national systems. Universities must prepare leaders and teachers. Especially must the graduate schools of education welcome to their seminars prospective leaders from other professions that these in their own turn may take better account of the educational bearings of their respective fields upon the public welfare. In all such preparation the chief aim must be the inclusive and intelligent social outlook and the correlative integrated educational outlook. The why of the adult education movement must produce its appropriate how. Great care must be taken to put the work in good hands. Too much is at stake and too delicate are the elements initially involved to trust the new adult education to any but the best.

THE PROFESSION AND THE NEW SCHOOL

AND last of all we come to our customary school work. On the newer social basis we must make over our whole traditonal system, elementary, secondary, and higher. Because space is lacking the discussion here will be limited to secondary education. Analogous treatment would be necessary for the rest.

The rethinking of secondary education is long overdue. For various causes we have been very reluctant to apply the results of better educational thought to the secondary school. The college is partly to blame for this, but parental prejudice and professional inertia must share the blame. In particular we must rethink secondary theory and practice to a more satisfactory social basis. Let us begin by comparing the present typical situation with our present best conception of what we wish. As here set down, the contrast is a bit too sharp. What-is in many places is already moving toward what-we-wish. But even so the contrast may perhaps help us to see better what changes are needed.

At present, school and society are, as regards the typical case, sharply and widely separated. Thought and action in the two realms are divorced in space, in time, and in kind. The school is housed in a building set apart, peculiar to its kind. This is but the outward and visible sign of an even greater inner difference. So far as concerns the best-recognized school activities, the ordinary school subjects, there is in them but little of life with its inherent thinking or the inherent testing of this thought by the inevitable ever-widening consequences to life. As most of the subjects are now conceived, it seems all but

55

impossible that the kind of thought here desired could find a place. Again—and still as regards the best-recognized subjects—there is, on the whole, but little connection between what is studied in school and what is going on in the world outside. There is all but no opportunity in these school subjects for these young people to share with their elders in actual social activities. School as conceived and defended is hardly, if at all, other than a supposed preparation for a future adult state. From this angle again are thought and action divorced, this time a decade or more. Effectual thinking—in terms of the relation of means to consequence—is thus again all but impossible. Also, social attitudes are in great measure limited either to the snobbish society-page sense of social, or to the maintenance of the social and economic *status quo,* or to the "rah rah" type of school spirit—all contrary to the social spirit we need. The curriculum, too, is largely bookish, often conventional and snobbishly "cultural." From the point of view of controversial issues and institutional criticism, the content is on the whole surprisingly "safe," and innocuous—mathematics, Latin, English classical literature, modern languages, general history, physics; typically no critical consideration of life's problems as the young face them. The final results, particularly in the northeastern part of the United States, are tested by examinations which in effect encourage cramming. Under all these circumstances any interest in the common good will hardly rise above a school spirit built to foster athletic victory. Only too frequently a pose of cynicism is the most obvious philosophy attained. Pupils attend secondary school very largely in order either to hold a present social status or to attain a status not as yet held by family. Overalls are accordingly despised by all. The white collar is the desideratum. So much for the typical secondary school as

56

we have had it. Fortunately, already there are many signs of a better day.

And now for a venture as to what we wish, a kind of ideal picture, something to aim at as we strive for a better day. Ideas, of course, will differ: the picture is the writer's own.

We wish ultimately that schooling shall reach into the thick of life itself, not social life as we now know it but that better kind we hope to have. In that life the young will have abundant opportunity at close association with the old. So far as possible the young will share with the old in considering and reaching responsible decisions. Through all such, both young and old alike will be building on the spot such social attitudes as seem after social consideration needed to care for the various matters undertaken. The whole population, young and old alike, will be consciously studying to criticize and improve society at any point of possibility and always for the common good. The thinking will always mean to lead to responsible consequences and will expect to test itself accordingly. On no other basis can thinking reach its best quality. Results will be tested by shared observable outcomes. All aspects of life—economic, ethical, esthetic—will be considered, as they occur, together, because all do in fact bear on each other. This is not to deny that any instance of these, or other matter of concern, may be taken aside, removed from its total setting, for temporary and more adequate study. But in all such instances the student himself will first have seen and felt the total setting and the relation of the part to this whole before the need to study the part alone can be felt.

Whether there will be in that distant day an actual school separately existing from the social process the writer would hardly care to hazard a venture. Let us suppose that there will be an educational center, somewhat like our present school where personal educational problems will receive especial attention, where also some who plan to specialize in scholarly work will have their working headquarters. But be this as it may, certainly the main bulk of education will be got in the pursuit of worthwhile social activities, especially, as suggested above, in company with the adults working vocationally along such lines. Child work, unlike our "child labor," will in that day be educative. Learning of all kinds will be inherent, intrinsic in life processes. The gain over what we now have will be incalculable. We can well imagine the people of that day looking back in wonder and pity at what we call education, that it was so formal, so impossibly remote, so futile.

One feature of that later day schooling we can well introduce much sooner, that is, a vocational guidance to suit the scheme of social planning.[1] By knowing the probable vocational needs of society, the school authorities can advise young people to wiser choices. Such a process need not be one simply of regard for individual welfare. A definite part of it will be to make for a juster wage scale. A proper guidance of the numbers to enter the various occupation groups can help the day when honest labor, socially needed, will carry the same remuneration wherever done. Our present scale of remuneration is fantastically antisocial and unethical.

Our task now is to look as far ahead as we can into the ideal future both of social life and of education, and ask what we can do to bring that ideal into being. In particular here, what kind of secondary school shall we set up next in order to move as rapidly as we can toward the ideal future life and the ideal future school?

[1] See Harold F. Clark, *Economic Theory and Correct Occupational Distribution.* Bureau of Publications, Teachers College, 1931.

As always, the ideal and aim is constituted of our best present anticipation of what we wish, so set before us as to furnish fruitful suggestions for the next steps to be tried. Some conceive of an ideal as a blue-print to be put into complete operation at once. Only rarely is this wise. Usually the transition must be more gradual. The ideal properly studied will give us direction of change and suggest specific changes. Simultaneously we study the present actual situation in order to find both possibilities of change and obstacles to such change. It is the part of wisdom to map such a consistent program of the road from where-we-are to where-we-wish-to-go as shall take due account of the three named factors: what we wish, what can now be changed, what cannot now be changed. Even so the program can at best be but tentative. Efforts seldom work just as planned. The aim itself usually looks different as we get closer to it. Means and end will thus always be under observation, we never know when further thought and experience will suggest wise changes. Our program must be fairly definite as to next steps, it will wisely be less definite as to the more distant steps. Here as always we shall expect to learn by experience.

The more general objectives for our new secondary school appear, then, to be to help society change for the better and to change the school accordingly, both together as fast as we can effect it, the school to change so as best to help society to change. In order to map out our educational program, we set before ourselves the actualities and the possibilities of the situation as follows. There are basic economic and political institutions which apparently demand urgent remaking. As we plan to make our pupils intelligent regarding such proposed changes we must expect both inertia and more active opposition. Desirably and probably, whatever changes are to be made will be made gradually and by orderly processes, not suddenly or violently. The new social planning apparently needed will come then gradually into effect. The schools, thus, must educate for intelligently directed social change rather than assume to inculcate the details of a specific program. The matter of indoctrination here suggested is so complex as to deserve special attention later. It suffices now to note simply that the proposed school program does not base itself on indoctrination. We have next to ask as to the more special school objectives for fostering such a developing process.

Along four general lines we shall expect to teach our pupils: (1) to expect social changes, that "becoming" is in fact the law of the life process, that wherever we look we see always something coming into being; (2) to wish the common good and seek it in season and out; (3) to learn to criticize in the light of the common good any existing and proposed institutions; (4) to seek to envisage a defensible social program, each thinking for himself and in behalf of the whole. Along these lines we shall seek to have the pupils enrich their lives on the best attainable basis.

More specifically, the school should give, eventually, say one-third of its time to avowedly socially useful activities. These will desirably reach out gradually into all social life. Presumably they will be run on a group activity or project basis. From these we shall hope that our pupils will get both valuable social attitudes and much direct knowledge of affairs. The effort will be—so far as young people can do it—to make social life better for all than otherwise it would be. At the first it will be necessary for more favored groups to avoid like poison any temptation to the Lady Bountiful attitude. In fact we have to admit that in our more favored sections as matters now stand, it will at first be difficult to find suitably educative activities

60

of the kind here desired. But they are so important that every effort must be made to find them.

Next, another third, possibly, of school time should be given to a study of social life and institutions. The beginning approach may be along two lines, one already made familiar by the unified social science approach of Dr. Harold Rugg,[1] the other taking its departure from the actual personal life and thought problems of the pupils. How these will develop is still in the lap of the gods. We lack experience at the present to tell with any certainty. An excellent promise seems to lie in the direction sketched by Dr. Goodwin Watson.[2] There should be definite effort to broaden and enrich the social interests of the pupils. Excursions and field trips will help supply actual touch. The work discussed just above will help at this point. The conscious effort will be that the pupils shall learn to criticize our institutional life. The historic approach will help to break up our all too dominant stereotype ideas.

These suggestions are, of course, given as tentative first steps. Actual trial will modify and add. We can lay aside any criticisms which might spring from a fear that conventional subjects will drop out—which would be no great loss—and even the weightier fear that these plans may not best accomplish the ends sought, but there is another objection we cannot refuse to consider.

EDUCATION AND PARTISANSHIP

THERE are those who assert that the program herein set forth is a partisan one, being simply the wish of a minor-

[1] *The Rugg Social Science Course,* 6 vols. New York, Ginn and Co., 1929-32.
[2] Goodwin B. Watson, "A New Secondary School," in *Progressive Education* 8:303-10, April 1931.

ity to shape society to its idea, and that any such use of the school is contrary to public policy, that the glory of the American school has been its avoidance of sectarian and partisan propaganda or indoctrination.

That the general position herein set forth is at present a minority view is quite true. Socially, there is, of course, nothing wrong in a minority view as such. It is of the essence of historic free speech that a minority shall have the right to present its views and, if possible, win a majority to them. A deceiving propaganda cannot be defended, but the fair exposition of merits (so that intelligence may have a better chance to judge and choose) seems the only defensible program for a free people. The question as to the schools, however, involves issues which cannot be here ignored. On the face of it the plan herein proposed may seem, and to many does seem, a significant departure from American practice and apparently also from American ideals. We must examine it.

Some who oppose what is here advocated take the position that the school has nothing to do with helping to inaugurate changes, that on the contrary it has always limited its work to the transmission of the accepted values of the group and should continue so to do. This conception as thus held seems to fit a static civilization where the change from one generation to the next is so small as, in comparison, to be negligible. Until quite recently, as history goes, this slowness was characteristic of the growth of culture the world over, and naturally the school has hitherto followed this rule. But our times are certainly different. Change is no longer negligible. In fact change has become so very significant a factor in our lives that the school could hardly ignore it even if it wished to do so.

How, for instance, shall we apply the term "accepted values" so as to find what the schools are to transmit with-

62

out running into the fact of change? Current social thinking shows its fundamentalists, its average attitudes, and its advanced thinkers, differing degrees of advance in thinking, each offering different values to the school. Which shall the school transmit? Shall we find the lowest common denominator of accepted values and teach only those? And if so, what shall we do about the probably better new values not included because some of the backward members of the groups still reject them? Can we ignore them or shall we call attention to them as having good backing but not yet general acceptance? And if the school itself is to take no positive notice of them, shall we allow pupils to ask questions about them or discuss them? And if we allow such, are we not therein helping to inaugurate change? It is difficult to see how alert teachers with alert pupils could entirely shut out newer ideas, and still more difficult to see why they should try to do so.

In connection with the foregoing it is further argued that while the school should not strive to introduce changes in ideas, it can and should teach such accepted values as open-mindedness, how to think, methods of study and attack and the like, so that when our pupils leave us they will be equipped for attack upon current problems. In reply we should have to ask how people learn open-mindedness? Whether one may be open-minded along one line and not another? Whether one does not have to deal openmindedly with the current social problems if he is to learn open-mindedness along that line? And so also with methods of attack and thinking in general. We need not accept the extreme restriction of "transfer" taught by some, but any reasonable consideration of what thinking means and of how we learn to think will show that familiarity with content is perhaps the chief factor in successful thinking. There are, to be sure, certain habits of stopping to examine, of suspended judgment and the like, but even these work best in those fields where we have appropriately built them up. Some of us connected with the universities during the war hysteria days will recall that the natural scientists on the whole acted about like average citizens in yielding to the hysteria, while the social scientists on the whole resisted the mania, at least in much greater degree. The latter had learned their open-mindedness and methods of attack in good part from a study of such popular frenzies and this in order to protect their own thinking against such. The open-mindedness of the natural scientists, on the other hand, had been learned in physics, chemistry and the like, so that they had little immunity from spy mania or pacifist persecution. It appears clear that we must learn our thinking in the field itself if the thinking is to function fruitfully. If our pupils are to learn how to deal with current controversial issues they must practice dealing with such controversial issues. Otherwise we have little to hope from their education.

The claim that our program is wrongly partisan, however, must face more serious questioning. That there are limits beyond which good teaching should not go in pushing a program we cannot deny. For one thing, the sensitivities and even the prejudices of parents cannot be disregarded. Teachers cannot hold everything in their hands. Other people need to be considered. No one rule can be laid down. Parents, for example, do not have the right—though probably most still claim it—to fix the future thinking of their children. Teachers have at times obligations to help children to free themselves from the limitations which ignorant parents have with the best of intentions attempted to fasten irrevocably upon them. But even in such instances the parents still have rights, and the thoughtful teacher will wish to respect them. Courtesy and regard for the feelings of others must never be forgot.

Often, also, the community as a whole is united in some prejudice. In such case prudence adds her voice to the admonitions of courtesy. The teacher who attempts to ride rough-shod over community sensitivities will in this country come, as a rule, to grief. The board members, being subject to election, will side with the community. The good teacher will recognize such a situation before it arises and act accordingly, and this not simply from prudence and kindly courtesy but also from a further consideration. If the teacher accept the point of view herein set out, he will make positive efforts to help the adult portion of the community as well as the school children to think more adequately about social matters. Once this attitude be taken, the teacher will know that to irritate and alienate the community is by just so much to hinder the program. The school people then will build their programs with the whole community in mind, knowing in particular that the first steps must be slow and highly considerate even of ignorant prejudices.

The question still remains, however, as to the actual classroom teaching. If we hold a social program before us as we teach, are we not engaging in partisan propaganda and indoctrination in a manner forbidden by best American ideals?

EDUCATION AND INDOCTRINATION

THIS problem of indoctrination is so complex and those who discuss it so easily get lost in the maze of definitions that we must pick our way here with care.

Originally education as an intentional process was precisely limited to handing down unimpaired the tribal customs, such customs, that is, as might suffer if they were not given special consideration. The presupposition to this educational practice was that neither elders nor youth might properly question what was thus handed down. Learn meant that the youth should accept and acquire what was authoritatively set before them. Teach meant the process of setting out the official tribal doctrines and customs and requiring the youth to learn them. Docility was the chief virtue of youth, as fidelity to tribal ways was that of the elders.

After letters came and philosophic doctrine was formulated in Greece, the schools, which had already become literary, now became formal, with, however, the same presuppositions underlying. Knowledge was not to be questioned, though it might be understood so as to be better learned. In any event it must be accepted. Learn still meant faithful acquisition. Teach still meant supervising and enforcing the process. With the coming of Christianity and orthodoxy, these presuppositions were even sharpened and made more rigid. In other respects knowledge and learning and docility kept their old definitions. Docility became even more surely a virtue.

With the Reformation orthodoxy became plural, but the presuppositions otherwise remained. Schools now became strictly partisan, with indoctrination their conscious policy. The aim was to fix our doctrine in our young— and in any others we could get access to—so that when they became old they would not depart from it. This was the education brought to America.

With the coming of American independence, the necessity of respecting many religious faiths and the general Deistic outlook among the leaders united to bring about the American doctrine of the separation of church and state. When state public schools became prevalent religious teaching was (nominally) excluded, and the ideal arose of impartiality before sectarian and partisan differences; so that in professed theory the public school avoids

66

indoctrination along any partisan line. Fairness has seemed to demand it.

Meanwhile another line of influence was developing within the social life of the people. Science and invention brought on industrialization. Changes within our institutional life became more numerous and immigration more divergent from the original stock. Two opposed reactions then arose, one to question tradition and criticize institutional life in the wish to facilitate changes along better lines, the other to fear and oppose change and cultural diversity and to seek accordingly to unify the nation on a crystallized American tradition.

Whereupon it became evident that the public school had never ceased to "indoctrinate," even in the matter of sectarian and partisan differences. The rule against indoctrination held only where old stock America was locally divided. Otherwise a different rule prevailed. By a sort of tacit agreement there has been presupposed in the opening exercises of our public schools, in the songs, holidays, text-books, and teaching emphases the united old stock outlook—the Protestant, Nordic, American democratic-republican, *laissez-faire,* capitalistic way of looking at things. The Bible (King James version) is often, if not commonly, read (certain states require it). Protestant Christian songs may be sung. Nordic superiority is assumed, any questioning of the perfection of our political and social institutions is taboo, socialism and communism may be denounced but hardly otherwise discussed. Programs are made on this basis, text-books are so written, teaching is so conducted. After the World War this hitherto more or less unconscious inculcation of the favored position became a more conscious policy. The Ku Klux, the American Legion, the D. A. R., the National Security League, and the like, virtually joined hands to establish in our schools a conscious and compulsory

67

system of indoctrination in what they proclaim to be the only true American tradition.

Against this obscurantist position another has meanwhile been at work, especially among the better educated. This claims to represent more truly the better American tradition as propounded by Franklin, Adams, Jefferson, Madison and Washington in favor of free speech and conscious study, but even more to represent the necessity of open study if in these shifting times we are to direct our policies in the light of intelligence. This position, admitting differences due to age, would encourage the frank investigation on the part of teachers, pupils and students of our social and political history and institutional life, believing that only from such open-minded study and investigation can the best education be got.

The proponents of this latter position are particularly impressed with the historic fact that most, if not all, of present-day approved institutions had at their inception to fight for a chance to live as against the opposition of the then *status quo* outlook. They think the like opposition is at work now. They freely admit that many worthless and even hurtful proposals are from time to time offered for acceptance, but they still hold that the open-minded discussion of any and all proposals on their merits seems the only reliable means by which to select the better from the worse. From this point of view that kind of education is to be sought which best makes for the habit and disposition of open-minded criticism with reliable skill in the process. Moreover—those of this position go on still further to assert—intelligent citizenship is impossible without such open study and criticism of institutional life, for intelligent action is impossible apart from an all-round knowledge of weaknesses as well as strengths. This position, accordingly, favors this open-minded study and rejects indoctrination (in the bad sense). The latter

68

it defines as any kind of education which sets out so to teach anything that later on it cannot or will not be questioned on its merits even if reasonable cause so to do should appear. Or, from another angle, indoctrination is any kind of education which does not intend so to teach as to make the learner a better independent judge of the matter under consideration. Thus has the "liberal" position hitherto opposed indoctrination.

More recently, however, a new line of thought has been presented. Some who wish to see adopted a thoroughgoing scheme of social planning have questioned the adequacy of the foregoing discussion of "indoctrination." These ask whether or not merely to be born and grow up in a given group does not inevitably indoctrinate one in the habits, customs and outlooks of that group and whether this is not good rather than evil, whether to fail so to indoctrinate would not leave the young without culture at all—than which no worse state could well be imagined. These go on further to ask whether, therefore, the most important of all problems is not as to the kind of culture which will be imposed upon the young, and whether, accordingly, education should not assume the task of helping to devise a better culture and teaching this openly and intentionally to the young. These ask, more specifically, whether or not there does not now go on in this country, partly unconsciously but partly intentionally, an actual indoctrination in outworn and now hurtful institutional forms and theories, particularly in the matter of the economic system, and whether it is not necessary for the educational profession, as of right and duty the protagonist of the best possible culture and civilization, to take effectual steps to supplant this hurtful indoctrination with a better. And they ask, still further, whether our ideal citizen is the impartial student of each new proposal that comes along. Is not the ideal citizen, on the contrary,

69

rather, one who feels values and has convictions so that he is ready to give himself to them, to work and fight for them if necessary? And amid such times as these, when selfishness sits entrenched in tradition, can men of insight rest in such scholarly impartiality? Must they not—teachers as well as others—so burn with conviction and zeal that they will seek in season and out to tear down the selfish tradition and build instead the needed tradition of supreme allegiance to the common good?

OPEN-MINDEDNESS AND CONVICTIONS

IT is impossible not to sympathize with the general purpose and attitude back of these questionings and to accept some of the argument. To begin with the last point, our situation is urgent. Tradition does bind. Convictions are needed. Action is imperative. Under such circumstances that outlook or disposition of philosophy would indeed be futile which so worships open-mindedness that it can reach no convictions, which remains so impartial that it can neither decide nor act. And it may justly be claimed that in the past too much of academic study has sinned in this direction. But there are implications here which we cannot accept. There seems to be supposed some sort of inherent opposition between thought and action, as if one must choose between the two, or as if the effectual man needs to curb his thinking propensities.

Thinking seems best taken as the anticipatory or preliminary phase of action, when we are tentatively trying things out before committing them to final action. On this basis there can be no incompatibility or opposition between thought and action. The two are but correlative phases in one continuous process. True enough, some think—in a fashion—and do not act, and others may act without adequate thought, but these are only bad habits of thinking-and-acting. Closer to our problem, there are some who begin on a course of action and stop too readily to reconsider, just as there are others who, having begun to act, refuse to reconsider even when probably good reasons for review arise. There is no rule in the matter. Intelligence will demand that a person be sensitive to possible demand for review and reconsideration. To persist in a plan just because it has been begun and in the face of proper reasons for reconsideration is not excellence, but the opposite. It is in effect simple stupidity.

Then, as we take up the matter at hand and face our present economic situation, the extreme probability is that this country—if it adopt either—will have a planning economy rather than a once-for-all planned economy. That is, if our country adopts planning, it will almost surely come to it gradually, and even when the scheme is in full operation, planning will be continually in process —just as Russia has all the while been revising its five year plan. Under such circumstances the disposition to be impartial in studying particular plans will be an asset. If one's convictions should make him persist in a plan after revision was indicated, we should count him not an ideal citizen but in so far a hindrance. And if his zeal should make him offer to fight for the same old plan, we should probably take active steps to curb him. With continual planning—and especially if, as previously argued, the process be democratic—there will ever be need for the group intelligence to be continually studying the situation, proposing and criticizing plans, adopting plans for trial, studying and criticizing the results, revising the plans in the light of results, and so on in unending succession. And as previously discussed, if this process is to be really efficient the whole people must engage in it, with all the types of leadership continually and mutually pushing forward the whole process. These things most fundamentally mean that such continual planning must run itself on an experimental basis and no other. In particular, intelligence must always be alert to criticize the process both as to ends set up and as to means used, and this intelligence must always be ready to review and if need be revise the previous plans and conclusions whenever new pertinent data sufficiently demand it. In other words, the good citizen will continually be called upon to help judge whether to persist in a plan now under way or to stop and review it. And his zeal and convictions should be subservient to the best intelligence he can find and not the other way about.

The question of zeal and conviction was in effect discussed earlier as the leadership of interest and concern. Without the leadership of zeal and conviction we can hardly hope to see any significant change introduced into our social and economic system. But when we propose to work for such zeal and conviction, and leadership along such lines, we are much concerned whether we are to count, as seems above implied, that zeal and conviction are opposed to thinking and the disposition to weigh things. Must these two pairs be opposed to each other, so that we have to give up thinking and weighing things if we are to have zeal and conviction? Is not the contrary true, that he who understands the bearings of any new proposal on the other things he holds dear is the man who most truly has convictions rather than prejudices? And does not the man of convictions stand the more steadily because he has a larger and better organized set of bearings back of his convictions? And is this man hurt in his efficient outlook because he understands the relative values of things and intelligently judges how much time and effort and cost a particular cause is worth in relation to other causes put in jeopardy by a proposed course of action? And does he not know, therefore, more defensibly when to yield and when to hold steady?

An understanding zeal is in fact the only kind we wish. We should fear to trust any other. How could we rely on citizens whose zeal is based on they know not what, perhaps chance or the mere say-so of some one else or on some "conditioning" done on them when they were too young to know what it was all about? It is an intelligent understanding which gives stability. History shows that the army which knows its cause and has a philosophy is in the long run far more efficient than any other. Applied intelligence, moreover, is our sole reliable basis for judging what cause to back. A zeal based on any other foundation would be a dangerous kind of zeal to have around.

DOES THE GROUP CULTURE INDOCTRINATE?

BUT there were other questionings of our discussion which we must consider. It was suggested that the group culture by an inevitable imposition indoctrinates the young in its customs, notions and ideals; that this is good and not evil, that for any one to miss such indoctrination of culture would leave him helpless beyond words. The term *indoctrinate* as here used demands scrutiny lest a meaning which only dubiously fits in this connection should surreptitiously commit us to a practice which we cannot otherwise or elsewhere approve.

That each group culture does profoundly affect the development of its young is beyond question. The influence is even deeper than the wording used implies, since to this process the child owes his very selfhood with also the initial content at any rate of his mind and character. And the process, as such, is accordingly good, nay invaluable. But is this process properly called indoctrination? This education from the group culture has two aspects, the one inherent in learning the culture so as to use it, the other dependent upon how the elders treat the matter. If the elders are dogmatic upholders of the cultural *status quo* and believe it should not be criticized, the children will likely accept the culture uncritically and tend later to hold to it against question. This kind of education we properly call indoctrination and these children will have been in so far indoctrinated. If, however, the elders think that the culture needs criticism and remaking and if they try so to deal with their children, then the young will less likely grow up dogmatists, that is, they will less likely be indoctrinated. Whether then the transmission of the group culture to the young be indoctrination or not will depend on how the elders manage the process, or, in another set of words, will depend on the character of the culture. The indoctrinating kind of culture will indoctrinate. The other kind will not, at least not so often nor in the same degree. After earliest infancy the mere transmission is not of itself indoctrination in any sense that we should care to distinguish.

Going on to a second question, we agree that the profession of education should share in the task of devising a better culture and help the young themselves to acquire a constructive attitude toward the process. We should, however, register certain reservations in order to guard against mistakes.

Clearly the profession of education should not assume the entire task of devising a better culture. It should, however, share in this task, and might well assume responsibility for being alert to all the significant educative effects involved.

Also, we should not assume that the young will learn the new culture solely or even chiefly through the ministrations of the profession of education. In fact the contrary is more probable, that any culture at any time is most and

74

best learned—and rightly so—by actual sharing in the social processes where that culture is at work. The profession of education should probably accept responsibility for the good working of such inherent educative effects, at least to the degree of being alert to what is thus taking place and calling effectual attention where better results might thus be attained. It seems, also, further proper that the profession of education should especially be conscious of the part the schools might and should properly play in promoting cultural changes. This book is an instance of the acceptance of such responsibility. There still remains, however, the problem of the degree to which we think the schools should select a particular social program and seek to teach it specifically to the pupils. This problem we are now ready to take up in connection with the further questioning of the social program herein set forth.

THE TEACHER AND HIS CONVICTIONS

THAT our schools now help to indoctrinate our pupils in outworn and now hurtful social and institutional beliefs and attitudes appears to be quite true. That a better school should work against this indoctrination and should besides take positive steps to help bring a better day is one of the underlying theses of this book. But the writer finds himself still unwilling to have our schools embark on any policy of partisan indoctrination, even in behalf of a course dear to himself. The reasons for this reluctance lie along two main lines; first, such indoctrination fails of giving the children what seems to be the highest available type of education; second, such a partisan indoctrination means that I approve a public policy for the schools when I and my party are in control but which I am unwilling to have put into operation when rival doctrines are in control.

75

If, then, I am teaching young people, I shall feel it my supreme duty to them that they shall grow in such fashion that they become more and more significantly sensitive to life about them, both its deficiencies and its possibilities, how to correct the former and how better attain the latter, believing that if they will so grow they will at one and the same time be both happier as individual persons and more effectually coöperative with others who are working for better things.

What shall I in connection do about my own convictions? Shall I use them in teaching these young people or shall I teach quite independently of what I think? If I really have convictions that matter to me I cannot possibly teach independently of them. They are an essential part of me. Does this mean that I shall set up my convictions as formulations which my pupils should accept and so "teach" them? It does not. That would not be education. I must know that there are difficulties here and I must guard against the dangers involved. I must use the best knowledge I have in helping my pupils to survey the field and to weigh the arguments. But I must be careful that my superior knowledge does not keep them from searching and thinking and concluding for themselves. Probably I must at some stage tell openly what I think, but I must so tell it and so couple other possibilities with it that my pupils are not unduly influenced to accept my position on any basis of authority. Otherwise, I am not making them independent and capable in thinking, or, more exactly, I am keeping them from really thinking and so from growing as they should.

If I teach in this manner, what hope have I that my pupils will think "as they should"? My hope is in the working of intelligent study. My pupils may not conclude what I have concluded. I am not properly working for that. What I should wish is that they shall so think while

I am helping them that they shall better think then and even better also later. As for concluding what I think, I may be wrong, I may myself think differently later. As I should not wish to tie my later thinking to my present conclusions, so I should not wish to tie their thinking to my present conclusions. I must wish them to grow even as I wish for myself to grow, and this even to the point of improving over what I now think.

I shall, accordingly, use my present best knowledge to help map out the field of study. In so doing I must avoid the extremes, on the one hand, of too broad a field so as to weary my pupils and waste their endeavors, and, on the other hand, of too narrow a field lest their vision be limited to a view that sees only the selected evidence that precisely supports my conclusion and they have no fair chance to study and judge for themselves. Also, I must help them to see as alternatives, the chief rivals to my conclusions. And similarly all through, what I have judged best at each stage and point must be the basis for mapping an area on both sides of my own thought process, neither too broad nor too narrow. For my pupils must study fairly and conclude accordingly, else I am not helping them the best possible.

This way of utilizing my best knowledge, yet so as not to indoctrinate my pupils, gives me my just defense when others would charge me with using my school access to foster in partisan fashion my own position. I have not "taught" my position. I have made my pupils study not so much it as an area. My position will be considered as one of the possible hypotheses, but always in comparison with other positions. I may even present the argument that influenced my own decision, but in such fashion that through it all my pupils have been helped to learn to think and decide for themselves. This, and not that they reach my decision, has been my aim. That I shall not entirely succeed in maintaining my intended fairness is but probable, but I must make the effort.

Some may ask whether this care to keep the teacher's conviction from affecting unduly the thought processes of the pupils may not deprive them of possibly the best part of an education, namely vision and zeal, vision of a worthy cause and zeal to pursue it. That there is danger need not be denied, but is it not fairer to charge the possible loss here rather to the attitude within the community than to the teacher? It is this which makes it a partisan matter. Because the parents feel as they do, the teacher cannot speak freely. His long-run effectual influence demands that he make manifest his fairness on the partisan question, even at some loss elsewhere. Even so he can present his position with its vision as one hypothesis for consideration, so that, even at the worst, there need be no total loss. Of course, if the parents were united in sharing the teacher's conviction, or if they were indifferent, he could work more effectually on the vision and zeal, though even then he should have to guard the pupils' thinking lest his position interfere there. The teacher's task in the face of partisan opposition is simply the common situation involving contradictory values. Do what he will, he cannot get all. He must act for the largest whole as best he can see it.

CONCLUSION

WE now conclude the special work of the profession of education. It has, first of all, broadened its own outlook beyond mere school-keeping to include a concern for significant educative effects wherever found. The profession will endeavor to use educative procedures to improve any such bad effects and to promote the better. In particular, considering the great significance of the present economic and social situation the profession will join forces with

78

other agencies in the effort to bring about such study of this situation as will mean an increasingly intelligent planning of the social and economic processes to the end that life may be better for all.

As a first step in such a program the profession must remake its own outlook so as to acquire one and all a truly social point of view. It should then undertake to secure the intelligent study of the social situation both in school and in the adult world in the light of the best that is known, that life may begin at once to be better. Life it must view as one continuous process, with education as the effort at its intelligent direction. Each period of life will show its problems. The aim of education will be to help those of each period so to study its problems that they will more surely act intelligently in both private and public affairs. All must come to expect social changes and adjust their thinking accordingly. If we are to meet the confronting situation, all must wish the common good. All must learn to criticize intelligently both existing and proposed institutions. And all must seek, each for himself, a unified outlook on life in place of the conflicts all too common within because they are so deeply at work without.

In particular, in order to help best in the adult world, a new and much more inclusive education must be planned with the aim of reaching all classes of the population in a serious study of life's problems and this in the hope that early steps may be taken to improve our institutional life. Such study among adults should help the schools greatly, partly in relieving the schools of the now impossible task of trying to give an education which will supposedly last for the rest of life. It should further help the schools by making parents and the community in general more intelligent as to what should go on in school and therefore more willing to have the schools undertake a really social program.

The school as we know it must be remade to a more social point of view. Now the aim is too often so to equip each pupil that he may the better get ahead of others. Content and method will need remaking. Much of what is now taught is too largely conventional and all too remote from life. The idea that education consists in the acquisition of stated subject-matter must give way to the study of problems vital within the lives of the young people and to the undertaking of enterprises significant within the community. Only in such way can we hope to get the needed intelligent thinking about social affairs or build adequate social attitudes. As far as the age of the pupils will permit they must become intelligently critical of our, and their, social life and institutions. It is, of course, true that there can be but inefficient social education by the school so long as the institutions of the social and economic world work directly against the effort of the school. But we can do better than we have been doing. With adults working to change our institutions for the better, there will come a better day for the school. When elders are critical of social life about us, that life will have less power to mis-educate the young. As fast as that social life can be changed, the school can become in its own processes more effectively educative. Working thus simultaneously with old and young we may hope to hasten the better day.

CHAPTER VI

SUMMARY AND CONCLUSION

*

THE SITUATION

CIVILIZATION is, perhaps, at one of its great turning points. Modern technology brings far-reaching changes and demands yet more. It has given us the means for creating unheard-of wealth, but it takes away the historic American dream of equal opportunity for individual freedom and initiative. The old frontier individualism is gone and with it must go our old competitive business. New arrangements must be achieved.

BUSINESS THWARTS TECHNOLOGY

As matters stand, technology is not allowed to serve as it might. The outworn business view prevents. Production must henceforth be made to balance in a complete circle, enough wheat to meet the need for wheat but no more, and so with all the rest. Distribution must balance production. The whole quota of wheat must be sold or farmers cannot buy their several quotas from the others, and so, also, with all the other producers. Prices and wages must suffice to move the whole varied production. Planning alone can do this. The rule of competitive rivalry is henceforth confusion and ruin. A planning technology could banish depressions and achieve economic security for all, even to abundance.

THE now outworn business system has become anti-social in its effects. As shown above, it refuses to let technology serve as it might. It brings recurrent depressions. It distributes wealth most unjustly; even in 1928 two-thirds of our population were held below the approved standard of living, while millionaires were being made overnight. The old system maintains a standing body of the unemployed running into many thousands and the numbers must greatly increase. Business as business cannot on the old competitive basis take account of the various inhuman effects which it entails; dividends and regard for the human element cannot be reconciled.

THE BAD EDUCATIONAL EFFECTS OF OUR BUSINESS SYSTEM

OUR business system brings, also, serious educative effects. Everything that a man does educates him. If he accepts inwardly what he does, he grows that way. In present business a man must work for himself. Rewards and approval so come. We then virtually pay our people to become selfish individualists, and many do. Look at the public indifference to bad political conditions. Actual business conditions have educated our people to be indifferent citizens.

There is still more. Business offers many opportunities to make money for nothing done in return. Speculation is an example, and "unloading" doubtful stocks and bonds on the unwary, not to mention many, many other "shrewd" practices. The longer people live by such, the worse their morals tend to become. The great fortunes made by such practices are much discussed. The idea spreads. Many wish they might do the like. The word goes round that "they all do it." Graft becomes common. Racketeering arises. Crime becomes an occupation. Politics becomes corrupt in selling favors and protection. "Machines" arise to take care of the traffic. It is all of one piece. Such demoralization is very widespread. Public dishonesty is an educative effect of these bad business practices.

THE MORAL OBLIGATION UPON THE PROFESSION OF EDUCATION

THE profession of education must concern itself with all these things. These mis-educative effects of business challenge education's essential reason for being. Why educate for honesty and citizenship if surrounding business practices will nullify the effort? Education, too, has always been deeply concerned with human welfare. If a bad economic system lowers the life of the people, education cannot be indifferent. It must join hands with civilization to make a better world.

To undertake this new task a wider conception of the profession of education is needed. We need to accept social responsibility for studying all significant educative effects. At times this new profession will call public attention to important effects. At other times, as this, it will assume a new mission. It must help in educative fashion our whole people to study the problem before us because a crisis confronts civilization.

THE NEW ADULT EDUCATION

IF we are to deal adequately with this and other problems of the rapidly growing modern world, we must devise new agencies of adult education. In the case before us we must

83

consciously undertake to get as much of our whole adult population as possible, studying every phase of the whole economic question, particularly as to the need of a fundamental reconstruction of the system; and if the answer to this be yes, then as to the means to be employed. This is not partisan propaganda of any prior chosen answers. While many of us have already reached convictions on certain of these points, it is still study that we are promoting, study that will help build an intelligent interest in the problem to the end that an aroused public interest may efficiently reach its own solution to the problem.

Each one of us must work wherever we can to spread such study, first with ourselves that we may be as intelligent regarding the matter as possible, then with our colleagues, and so on out to the parents of our pupils, friends, and citizens in general. Discussion groups will perhaps help most. Lectures and forums will be useful. In season and out we work for the cause.

Our higher institutions must take up the work to prepare leaders and workers. Courses must be opened in adult education. Private organizations and public authorities must assume the wider work of organizing adult education on an effectual basis to carry on the work permanently. Now that civilization is in continual change and new problems ever arise, continuing education of grownups must become a permanent feature of our total educational system.

THE NEW SCHOOL

BUT the new profession will owe a newly conceived duty to the schools. We have always professed that we were educating for society, but our work has been largely conventional and quite in keeping with our hitherto individualistic point of view. We must now go further. The new

84

view demands a new social emphasis. We must study, according to age, current social problems as close to life as we can get them. This will often mean controversial issues, for we cannot keep off of them nor would we if we could. For our youth must learn to study and criticize our actual institutional life. Also, we must do all that in us lies to get our pupils and students at work at socially significant undertakings. The pupils of a small city might, for example, undertake an actual city planning project. They could study the city as a whole and map out a specific program of things which they as pupils might feasibly undertake, some to promote among the citizens, others to do themselves. Wisdom will have to be used in deciding what to undertake—that will be one of the educative aspects of the problem. The chief returns will be the social attitudes built from the acceptance of social responsibility and the development of social intelligence from working out the various subordinate projects. If the social implications of it all be studied as fully as age and experience warrant, these with the other results should bring rich returns in building effectual social outlook and attitude.

In such ways and more may a real profession of education come gradually into being that can hope to take effectual part in remaking our social structure and life. The demand is already upon us. Opportunity beckons.

88

Mis-education, social, from our economic system, 18-29 (Chapter III), 42; from business, 19-24, 82, 83; against study of *status quo*, 18, 27-29; political effects, 25-26; disregard of the workers, 26-27; disregard of good life, 27
Moral conditions. *See* Mis-education, social.
Moral conflict, within society, 19-20
Mussolini, referred to, 32

National Chamber of Commerce, plan of, referred to, 12
National planning board, suggested, 39-40. *See also* Social Planning.
National Security League, referred to, 67

Oil scandal, 18-19, 24
Open-mindedness, how taught, 63-64; in relation to convictions, 70-72

Parasitic gain, how demoralizing, 20, 82-83
Partisanship in teaching, 61-65, 75-78. *See also* Convictions; Education; Indoctrination.
Personality, disregarded by economic system, 26
Philosophy of life, gives stability, 72-73; new one now needed, 52-53
Pioneer America, 6
Planning. *See* Social planning.
Political conditions, how business corrupts, 18-19, 25-26, 32, 83; public indifference, 19, 21. *See also* Graft; Mis-education; Racketeering.
Production, needs proportioning, 13, 40, 81; no over-production, 13. *See also* Industrial system; mass production.
Profession of education, defined, 44-46; requires new definition, 45-46, 78-79, 83; duty to the expert, 47; must become socially minded, 47 ff., 79; must re-think educational theory, 48-49, 80; social responsibility, 46-47, 48, 62-63, 74-75, 78-79, 83, 85; requires better organization, 49. *See also* Adult education, a new; Education; Teacher.
Profit motive. *See* Economic system. *Also* Profit motive and human nature.
Profit motive and human nature, discussed, 14-17, 18; effect of economic system, 14, 16-17, 18. *See also* Economic system; *Laissez-faire.*
Program of education. *See* Educational program.

Psychological hedonism. *See* Profit motive and human nature.
Public mind, steered "safely," 28
Public morality, fostered by planning, 42; lowered by our economic system, 19 ff., 82-83
Public spirit, lowered by economic system, 21

Racketeering, referred to, 19, 24, 83; continuous with speculation, 23
Re-education. *See* Vocational education.
Revolution, violent improbable, 32
R. O. T. C., referred to, 16
Rugg, Harold, referred to, 61
"Rugged individualism," referred to, 9, 12
Russian five-year plan, 71. *See also* Communism.

School, needs social remaking, 55-61, 80, 84-85; too remote from life, 49, 54, 55; slights social question, 28, 56; moral efforts nullified by business, 24, 80, 83; new objectives, 59-80; should foster progress, 62-63; socially useful activities, 60-61, 80; study of social problems, 61, 80, 85; partisanship, 61 ff.; indoctrination, 65-78; teaching one's convictions, 70, 75-78. *See also* Education; Educational program; Profession of education.
Schwab, Charles, referred to, 9
Security, denied under existing conditions, 12; possible under planning, 13, 81
Shared search, the method of democracy, 33 ff., 40, 42. *See also* Group thinking.
Shaw, George Bernard, referred to, 46
Social planning, discussed, 30-31, 33, 39-41, 47; referred to, 3-4, 12, 42; possibilities of, 13, 81; to be gradual and continuous, 40, 59-60, 71-72; leadership in, 33 ff., 47; difficulties of, 40; some possible lines of, 39-41. *See also* Democracy; Education and social planning.
Social questions, slighted in school, 28-29; opposed by many, 18, 24, 27 ff., 49, 52-53, 54, 67-68
Speculation. *See* parasitic gain.
Standard of living, advancing in America, 6; in pioneer days, 7; low in 1928, 82
Study, opposition to, from selfish interests, 18, 24, 27 ff., 54; from the public, 49, 52-53; from super-patriots, 28-29, 67.
Swope plan, referred to, 12

89

Success, in pioneer days, 6; in the industrial era, 6, 24
Super-patriotism, 16, 28-29, 67

Tammany, referred to, 19
Teachers, most timid of professionals, 28; must consider communities. 64-65. *See also* Profession of education.
Technological unemployment. *See* Unemployment; Vocational education.
Technology, effect of, 9 ff., 81; misdirected by business, 81; possibilities of, 13, 81. *See also* Industrial system; Social planning.

Textbook assignments, condemned, 48
Tribal motives, group centered, 16-17

Unemployment, referred to, 11-12; insurance, 12, 41; standing, 82; technological, 41

Vocational re-education, 12, 41, 58
Vocational guidance, part of social planning, 41, 58

Wages, regulation of, 12, 58
Washington, George, referred to, 68
Watson, Goodwin B., referred to, 61
Workers' Education Association, referred to, 54

DATE DUE

JUL 7			
JUL 1 5			
SEP 2 7			
OCT 2 8			
JAN 2 8			
MAR 3 1			
OCT 2 2			
NOV 3			
MAY 1 7 1988			
DEC 0 7 1998			
GAYLORD			PRINTED IN U.S A.